ACCA

Paper P7 UK

Advanced audit and assurance

Pocket notes

ACCA APPROVED PUBLISHER

KAPLAN PUBLISHING

British library cataloguing-in-publication data

A catalogue record for this book is available from the British Library.

Published by:
Kaplan Publishing UK
Unit 2 The Business Centre
Molly Millars Lane
Wokingham
Berkshire
RG41 2QZ

ISBN 978-1-84710-598-1

Printed in the UK by CPI William Clowes Beccles NR34 7TL

Contents

The content and style of the exam

You will be given 15 minutes reading and planning time before this 3 hour exam.

Section A (50-70%) - 2 compulsory questions

- this section is compulsory and contains mainly 'case study' type scenarios
- a range of topics, issues and requirements can be addressed here (e.g. what are business risks, steps to be taken at the planning stage, and ethical considerations)
- it is vital that your answers address the specifics of the case scenario.

Section B (30-50%) - choice of 2 questions out of 3

- these questions will have more focus on specific topics (e.g. 'auditor's reports', 'professional ethics')
- there will be less scenario content than in Section A
- current issues will be examined across a number of questions.

Questions in both sections will be almost entirely discursive although there may be a need to assess materiality and calculate relevant ratios where applicable.

Aim of the paper

To ensure that candidates can exercise judgement and apply techniques in the analysis of matters relating to the provision of audit and assurance services and can evaluate and comment on current practices and developments.

The keys to success in Paper 7

- Try to provide all sides to an argument in your answers but be sure to conclude - at the end of the day professional accountants are looked upon to provide solutions to problems.

- You should try to discuss issues at as high a level as possible - put yourself in the position of the audit partner or senior manager of a company.
- Don't merely describe the scenario in answering questions - but analyse the points from the scenario and the implications, referring to relevant professional and technical standards as appropriate.

chapter

1

Regulation in a global economy

In this chapter

- Main sources of regulation.
- Public oversight and corporate governance.
- Board structures.
- Audit committees.

The main sources of regulation

The APB is the UK and Ireland auditing standards setter. It issues ISAs (UK and Ireland) and also establishes standards and guidance on assurance services that relate to activities reported in the public domain, Ethical Standards (ESs) in relation to independence, objectivity and integrity and advances the public understanding of auditing and assurance standards.

IFAC issues auditing standards through its standing committee, the International Auditing and Assurance Standards Board (IAASB), whose mission is to establish high quality, assurance, quality control and related services standards to develop the harmonisation process worldwide.

ACCA's Code of Ethics and Conduct

IFAC's Code of Professional Ethics

Public oversight and corporate governance

Corporate governance is about ensuring that public companies are:

- managed effectively
- for the benefit of the company and its shareholders.

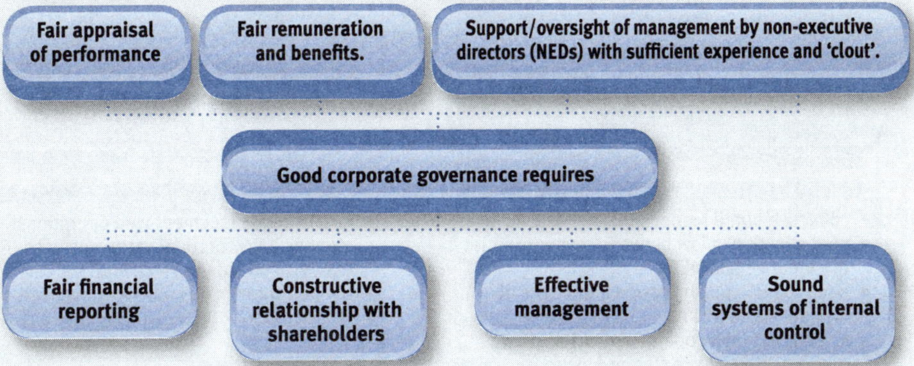

Good corporate governance can be enforced:

- by law – e.g The Sarbanes-Oxley Act, USA
- by agreement through codes of best practice – e.g. The Combined Code, UK, or
- through a combination of the two.

Board structures

Unitary board structure

UK & IRELAND

+ jurisdictions with comparable systems of company law

- collective board responsibility
- no distinction in law between responsibilities of executive and NEDs
- need to distinguish between functions of executive and NEDs
- need to establish board committees to monitor and act on different functions

Supervisory board structure

US

+ similar jurisdictions

- executive management with operational responsibility for running the business –CEO CFO, vice presidents, etc., and
- the board which has purely an oversight role

Audit committees

The Combined Code requires companies to have an Audit Committee consisting of at least three non-executive members with clearly written terms of reference. Key revision points:

Objectives

- Increase public confidence in credibility and objectivity of published financial info.
- Assist directors in meeting their responsibilities in respect of financial reporting.
- Strengthen the independence of the external auditor.

Advantages:

- Improve quality of management accounting
- Improved communication between directors, external auditors and management
- Avoids conflicts between auditors and management

Main functions include:

- Review of company internal control procedures.
- Review of internal audit function.
- Review of external auditors results to ensure audit has been carried out efficiently, effectively and independently.
- Recommending remuneration and nomination of auditors.
- Reviewing requirements satisfied under Combined Code.

Disadvantages:

- Fear purpose to "catch out" management
- Overburdening of non-executive directors
- May lead to "two-tier" board
- Costly

chapter

2

Code of ethics and conduct

In this chapter

- ACCA code and IFAC code.
- Threats and safeguards.
- Confidentiality.
- Conflicts of interest.

ACCA Code of ethics and conduct and IFAC code of ethics

Fundamental principles

The code identifies five fundamental principles in professional conduct.

- **Integrity**: Members should be straightforward and honest in all professional and business relationships.
- **Objectivity**: Members should not allow bias, conflicts of interest or undue influence of others to override professional or business judgements.
- **Professional competence and due care**: Members have a continuing duty to maintain professional knowledge and skill at a level required to ensure that a client or employer receives competent professional service based on current developments in practice, legislation and techniques. Members should act diligently and in accordance with applicable technical and professional standards when providing professional services.
- **Confidentiality**: Members should respect the confidentiality of information acquired as a result of professional and business relationships and should not disclose any such information to third parties without proper and specific authority or unless there is a legal or professional right or duty to disclose. Confidential information acquired as a result of professional and business relationships should not be used for the personal advantage of members or thirc parties.
- **Professional behaviour**: Members should comply with relevant laws and regulations and should avoid any actior that discredits the profession.

APB fundamental principles

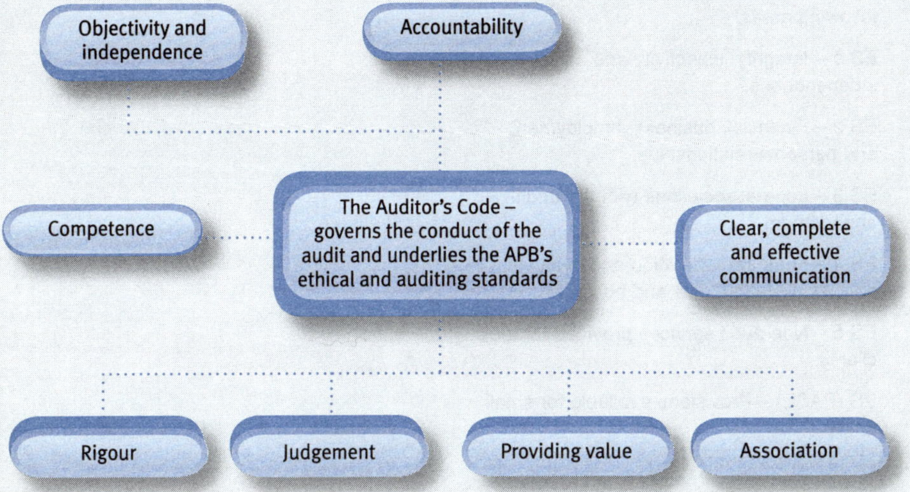

APB ethical standards

The APB Ethical Standards cover the following areas:

ES 1 – Integrity, objectivity and independence.

ES 2 – Financial, business, employment and personal relationships.

ES 3 – Long associations with the audit engagement.

ES 4 – Fees, remuneration and evaluation policies, litigation, gifts and hospitality.

ES 5 – Non-audit services provided to audit clients.

ES (PASE) – Provisions available for small entities.

Threats and safeguards

Members are required to apply the conceptual framework to identify threats to compliance with the fundamental principles, to evaluate their significance and, if such threats are other than clearly insignificant, to apply safeguards to eliminate them or reduce them to an acceptable level such that compliance with the fundamental principles is not compromised.

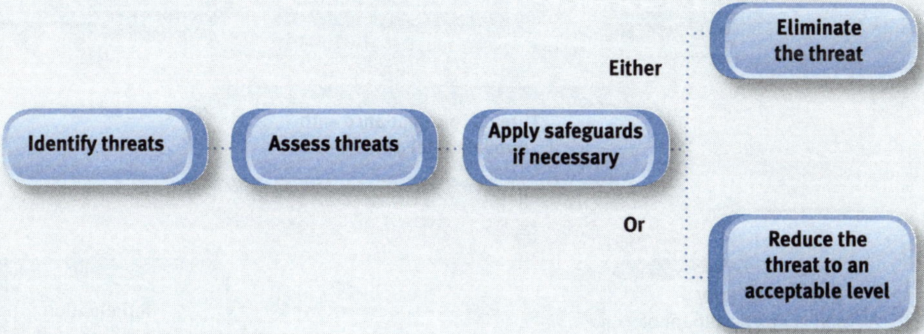

Threats

The ACCA Code sets out the broad range of categories that the threats fall into:

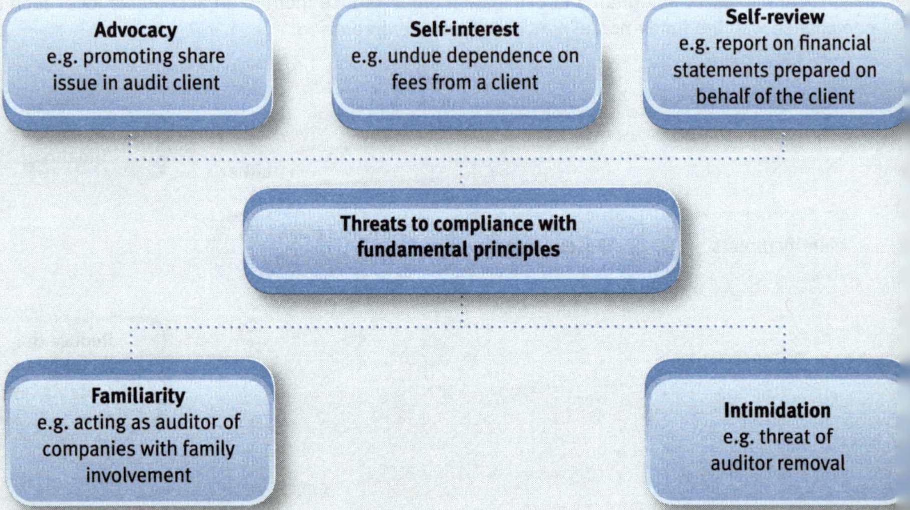

Safeguards

Safeguards can be classified into the following broad categories:

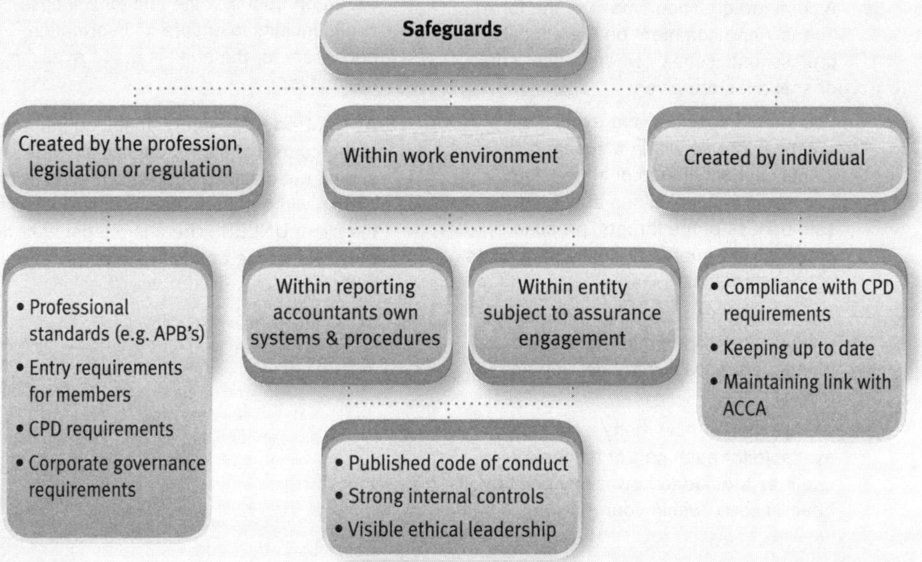

Exam focus

- A common question type is of the form "identify and comment on the ethical and professional issues", where a scenario, or scenarios are given.
- You should consider and explain all potential threats within a scenario, identify actions that should be taken in coming to conclusions about the seriousness of the threats, propose potential safeguards and ultimately what actions should be taken.
- You must expand on all of these areas – simply identifying that there is a threat to independence will not get you any marks!
- Always look at how many marks are available for each part of a scenario – use it as a guide to how many points you need to cover within your answer.

Confidentiality

Role: The auditor-client relationship is based on trust that the auditor will observe confidentiality to ensure all information necessary for the audit is made available to the auditor.

ACCA Code: Members acquiring information in the course of their professional work should not disclose such information to third parties without first obtaining permission from the client UNLESS there is a legal right or duty to disclose or it is in the public interest to do so.

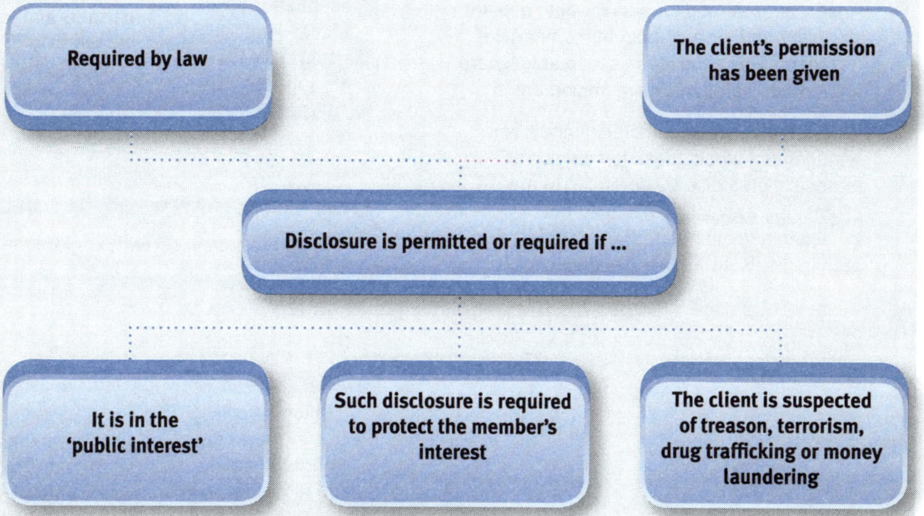
Required by law
The client's permission has been given
Disclosure is permitted or required if ...
It is in the 'public interest'
Such disclosure is required to protect the member's interest
The client is suspected of treason, terrorism, drug trafficking or money laundering

Conflicts of interest

Arise where an auditor acts for both a client company and for a competitor company of the client. This situation is acceptable where appropriate safeguards are implemented.

Where the acceptance/continuance of an engagement would, despite safeguards, materially prejudice the interests of any clients, the appointment should not be accepted/continued, or one of the appointments should be discontinued.

Conflict resolution

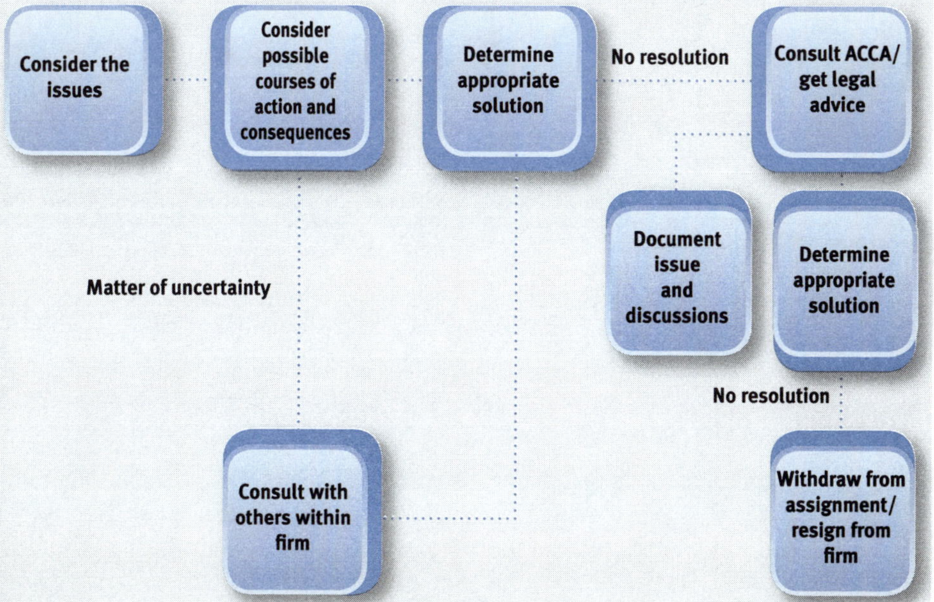

chapter

3

Professional appointments

In this chapter

- Professional appointment.
- Accepting new work.
- Documentation.

Professional appointment

Rules

- Clients are free to choose their auditor, or other advisors, and to change them as they wish.
- Members invited to act as an auditor by clients must contact the existing auditor to ascertain if there are any matters they should be aware of when deciding whether or not to accept the appointment.

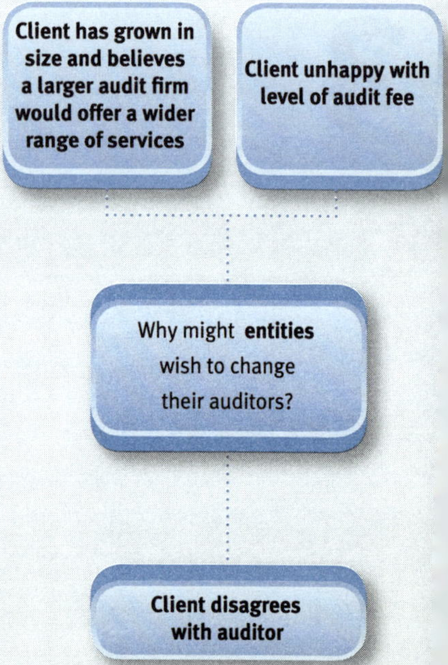

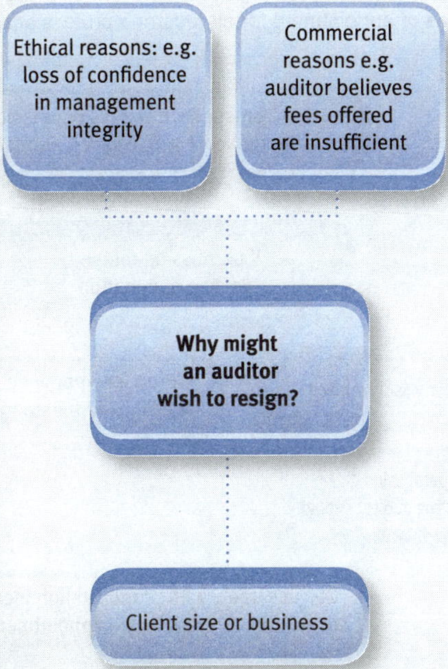
Ethical reasons: e.g. loss of confidence in management integrity
Commercial reasons e.g. auditor believes fees offered are insufficient
Why might an auditor wish to resign?
Client size or business

Procedures necessary before accepting a new client (where the organisation previously had an auditor. Same principles apply in respect of changes of appointment for all recurring professional work).

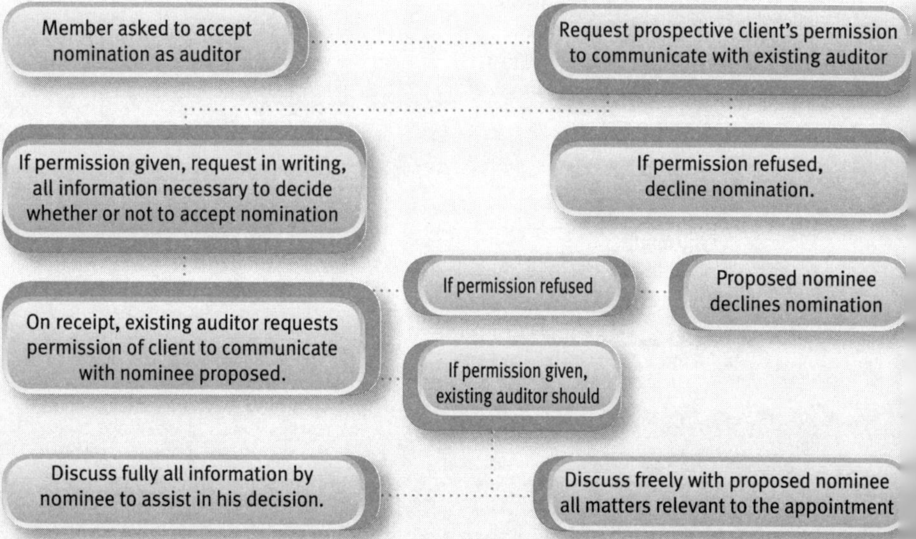

Documentation

'Documentation' relates to all the books, documents and papers, be they in electronic or hard copy, that the auditor collates/creates as audit evidence.

Clients have no right to demand access to documentation belonging to auditors, although the auditor may decide to allow access

All audit documentation is subject to the confidentiality rules discussed earlier

Documentation general principles

Documents belonging to clients must be returned to them or their agents or may be disclosed to a third party except where a **right of lien** is applied

General lien ... relates to repayment of all amounts outstanding irrespective of whether they relate to particular property. **RARE**

A 'right of lien' is creditors right to retain possession of a debtor's property until the debtor repays the creditor

Particular lien... relates to a particular debt in respect of particular property. Special circumstances must apply for a particular lien.

Exam focus

- The acceptance of a new client or engagement might be rolled into a wider ranging question regarding ethics.
- In such a question, always consider what steps an auditor must take to ensure that they are acting according to the fundamental principals – it is usually not just about whether previous auditors reply to your request for information!

chapter

4

Quality control

In this chapter

- Quality control.

Exam focus

- Included in the pilot paper as a multi-part scenario
- You will most likely be required to explain the weakness/es in a scenario and link it to failings both generally and in the quality control process of the firm, using the main areas identified in ISQC1.

APB quality control guidance

Quality control procedures will differ in nature between large and small audit firms.

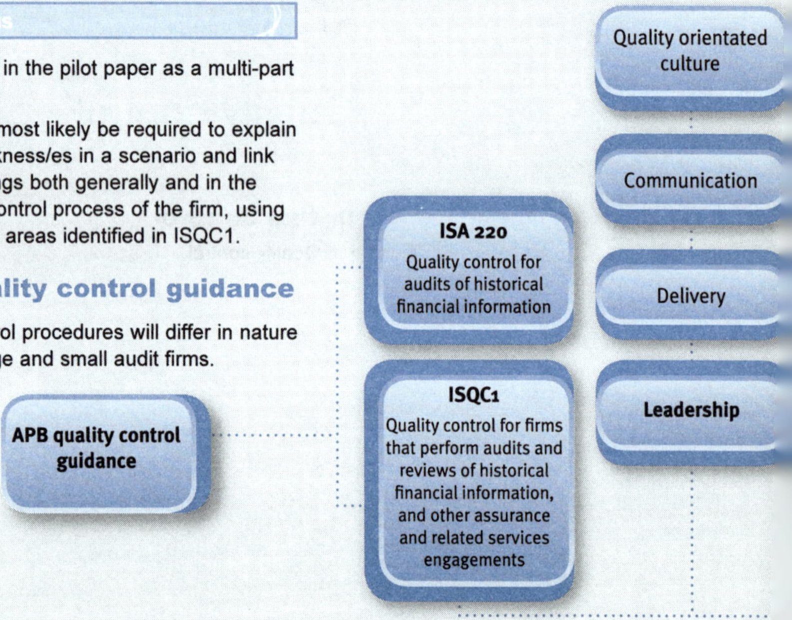

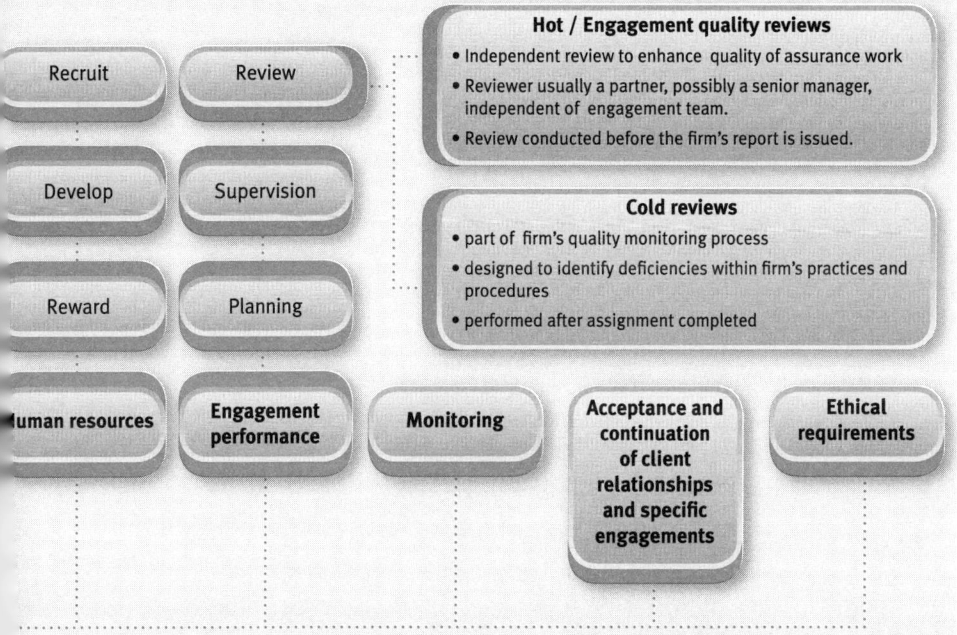
Hot / Engagement quality reviews
• Independent review to enhance quality of assurance work
• Reviewer usually a partner, possibly a senior manager, independent of engagement team.
• Review conducted before the firm's report is issued.
Cold reviews
• part of firm's quality monitoring process
• designed to identify deficiencies within firm's practices and procedures
• performed after assignment completed
Recruit
Develop
Reward
luman resources
Review
Supervision
Planning
Engagement performance
Monitoring
Acceptance and continuation of client relationships and specific engagements
Ethical requirements

chapter

5

Obtaining professional work

In this chapter

- Obtaining professional work.
- Tendering.

Obtaining professional work

Obtaining professional work

Advertising and publicity

ACCA Code of Ethics and Conduct

This material must not:

- Bring disrepute to the ACCA
- Discredit services offered by others
- Be misleading
- Fall short of any advertising codes

Fees

ACCA Code of Ethics and Conduct

- Basis of calculating fees should be pre-agreed and mentioned in the Engagement Letter to avoid contention
- Fees should be charged bearing in mind factors such as staff seniority, expertise, time spent, apportionable overheads, risk involved
- Contingency fees should be avoided except customary (e.g. insolvency work)

Tendering

Tendering

Definition

Tendering: the process of quoting a fee for work before it is carried out. This has lead to increased competition within the audit marketplace.

Audit firms have reacted by:

- merging to become more efficient, with the Big Four now dominating the market
- adopting risk-based auditing to reach the audit opinion in a more efficient manner
- attempting to increase their overall revenue by offering other services where possible (although there are some restrictions to offering other services by Ethical Guidance and Sarbanes-Oxley where applicable).

Matters to consider.

- Resources
- Competences
- Independence
- Risks
- Specialist skills
- Potential for profitability
- Additional services

Advantages of tendering	Disadvantages of tendering
• More efficient auditing • Auditing can be a loss leader	• Loss of long-term relationships of clients with auditors' • Market choice reduced by increased concentration • Lowballing • Companies may constantly change auditors to reduce costs further

Risks of tender include: wasted time, setting an uncommercial low fee, making unrealistic claims/promised in order to win the contract.

What goes in a proposal

- The basis of the fee.
- Nature, purpose and legal requirements of an audit.
- Client requirements and how the audit firm will meet them.
- Audit methodology.
- Outline of firm and personnel.
- Assumptions made, e.g. deadlines, geographical coverage, work performed by client.
- Ability of firm to offer other services.

Potential clients will assess tenders with the following relevant criteria.

- Clarity.
- Relevance.
- Professionalism.
- Personal/standardised.
- Timeliness of delivery.
- Originality.
- Range of other services.
- Reputation.
- Ability to deliver.

chapter

6

Professional legal issues

In this chapter

- Laws and regulations in an audit of financial statements.
- Money laundering.
- Fraud and error.
- Responsibilities for fraud and error.
- Auditor liability issues.
- Misconduct.
- Expectation gap.
- PII.

Laws and regulations in an audit of financial statements

ISA 250 Consideration of Laws and Regulations in an Audit of Financial Statements covers illegal acts by the client company.

Director's responsibilities	Auditor's responsibilities
• To ensure the entity complies with relevant laws and regulations. • To establish effective arrangements for preventing and detecting non-compliance.	• To obtain sufficient appropriate audit evidence about compliance with the laws and regulations that determine the form and content of the FS, and with those laws and regulations which provide a framework within which the entity conducts its business. • To plan and perform the audit with an attitude of professional scepticism recognising the audit may reveal conditions/events that would question whether an entity is complying with laws and regulations. • To consider risk of non-compliance with laws & regulations when seeking management representations & forming their audit opinion.

Reporting non-compliance

To management
Without delay!

To shareholders
Consider implication on audit opinion – possible disagreement or limitation of scope.

To third parties
Need to bear in mind duty of confidentiality but also duty to public interest.

Money laundering

Definition

Money laundering: process by which criminals attempt to conceal the true origin and ownership of the proceeds generated by illegal means.

Money Laundering

Legislation

- Criminal Justice Act 1993
- Terrorism Act 2000
- Proceeds of Crime Act 2002
- Money Laundering Regulations 2003

Offences

- Money laundering
- Tipping off
- Not setting up procedures
- Not complying with procedures

Relevant businesses

- Includes accountants

Ethical guidance

- Conflict re. confidentiality

Duties

Client identification

- Know your client
- Client due diligence

Appointing a MLRO

- With specified responsibilities

Staff training

- For all relevant personnel

Reporting

- Internally to MLRO
- Externally to NCIS

Basics of a client system

- To enable auditors to review client anti-money laundering procedures

Client identification

- Client identification and verification is a key component of 'know your client' (KYC) information:

Typical Client Identification Procedures

For an individual

Establish the client's full name and address.

Examine:

original documents

recent

utility bills

driving licence

passport.

For a company

Obtain copies of the following from the registrar:

certificate of incorporation

register of directors

register of members/ shareholders

registered address

For a trust

Examine trust deed.

Ascertain :

identities of trustees and beneficiaries

the purpose of the trust

sources of funding.

Basic elements of an anti-money laundering programme

Auditors, should ensure that the following basic elements exist in the client's anti-money laundering programme:

- dedicated resources
- written policies and procedures
- timely escalation and resolution of matters
- explicit management support
- sufficient training and education
- regular review/audit of the programme.

Relevant businesses

In broad terms the relevant businesses subject to the requirements of MLR 2003 are:

- businesses in regulated investment activities
- banking and bureau de change activities
- estate agencies
- tax advisors
- insolvency practitioners
- accountants and auditors
- providers of legal services
- businesses involved in the formation, operation or management of trusts and companies
- casino operators
- dealers in goods (if a transaction involves accepting a total cash payment of 15,000 euro or more).

Exam focus

- A question on money laundering is included in the pilot paper, and shows the type of scenario based question that might be asked.
- Some explanation of what you understand by money laundering may be required.
- Scenario will require you to identify potential issues and explain what the implications are for both the client and the auditor, including what actions should be taken and risks of non-compliance.

Fraud and error

ISA 240 the auditor's responsibility to consider fraud in an audit of financial statements

Fraud = intentional acts of deception

(May involve falsification of documents and records, misappropriation of assets, or misapplication of accounting policies)

Error = unintentional misapplication

Of accounting policies, oversights or misinterpretations

Management primarily responsible for the prevention and detection of fraud and error through the implementation and operation of adequate accounting and internal control systems.

Responsibilities for fraud and error

Responsibilities for fraud and error

Management
primarily responsible for prevention and detection of fraud and error

Management should:
- place a strong emphasis on fraud prevention and error reduction
- reduce opportunities for fraud to take place
- ensure the likelihood of detection and punishment for fraud is sufficient to act as a deterrent
- ensure controls are in place to provide reasonable assurance that errors will be identified
- foster, communicate and demonstrate a culture of honesty & ethical behaviour
- consider potential for override of controls or manipulation of financial reporting
- implement and operate adequate accounting and internal control systems.

Auditor
responsible for detecting misstatement where it affects the "true and fair view" "watchdog, not a bloodhound"

Not primarily responsible for prevention or detection of fraud or error within an entity, but do have an important role to play.
- Concerned with both fraud and error as either can cause material misstatement in the FS on which the auditor gives an opinion.
- Are not responsible for preventing, or detecting, fraud and error.
- Annual audit may act as a deterrent.
- Try to obtain reasonable assurance that there are no material misstatements in the FS
- Risk of not detecting material misstatement resulting from a fraud is higher than that relating to an error, as, it may be carefully hidden.
- ISA 240 requires auditors to consider the risk of material misstatement due to fraud for each entity, and to design and perform audit procedures to address that risk.

Exam focus

- The whole area of professional responsibilities is an area that is highly examinable .
- With the recent scandals and the impact they have had on the whole regulatory environment, including auditing standards, the professional responsibility and liability of the auditor is very topical.
- Be prepared to outline the major issues involved and to provide your own insight where asked.

Procedure where fraud or error is suspected

Consider potential effects – material or not?

If material, consider modified or additional procedures

Consider implications for the audit
- **Does the preliminary risk assessment need revising?**
- **How reliable are the management representations?**

Communicate with management

REPORTING FRAUD AND ERROR

To management:
- Auditor should report to those charged with governance where fraud or error discovered.
- Care must be taken to report to the appropriate level if auditor suspects management involved.
- Auditor should take legal advice.

To users of audit report:
- Should report to users to extent "true and fair view" is affected.
- Auditor may consider resigning in extreme circumstances or where entity does not take remedial action regarding the fraud. Legal advice should be taken.

To regulatory and enforcement authorities:
- Auditor's duty of confidentiality prevents him from reporting to third parties without client's permission – in certain circumstances, this duty is overridden by law or by the need to protect the public interest. Legal advice should be taken.
- Other matters to consider when justifying disclosure to authorities include the likelihood of repetition, the extent to which the public are effected and the gravity of the matter.

Auditor liability issues

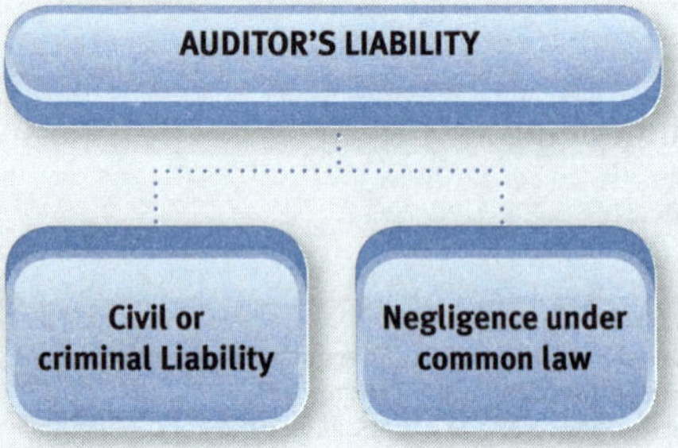

The specific duties of an auditor will be laid down in the relevant national legislation, but will include the general duty to report on whether the financial statements show a true and fair view, or similar.

In most countries liability can be classified under civil and criminal liability or liability under common law for negligence.

Civil and/or criminal liability is normally in relation to such matters as acting as auditor when ineligible, theft and deception, insider dealing, etc.

Auditors may be liable:

- to third parties suffering loss as a result of their relying on a negligently prepared audit report
- under insolvency legislation to creditors
- under fiscal legislation
- under financial services legislation
- under stock exchange legislation or rules.

Criminal liability can arise:

- when accepting an appointment if ineligible
- if property is misappropriated, financial advantage gained by deception, records falsified or deliberately publishing a misleading statement
- on insider dealing
- on other financial services legislation e.g. knowingly or recklessly making false statements in connection with an issue of securities.

For the auditor to be found liable to a third party:

A duty of care must exist

The auditor must know, or should have known, that the injured party was likely to rely on the financial statements

The injured party must have sufficient 'proximity' i.e. he must belong to a class likely to rely on the financial statements

The injured party must in fact have so relied

The injured party must show that he would have acted differently if the financial statements had shown a less attractive picture.

Solutions to the negligence problem

- Improved quality control.
- Impose a financial cap on liability.
- Professional indemnity insurance.
- Limiting liability by incorporation.
- Limited liability partnerships.
- The use of disclaimers.
- Many negligence claims are settled before they reach court.

Expectation gap

The gap that exists between what the public, especially users of financial statements, believe auditors do (or ought to do) and what the auditors actually do. It can split as follows:

- a standards gap
- a performance gap
- a liability gap.

Potential ways of closing the gap

- Users having a better understanding of the meaning, purposes and limitations of financial statements and the audit report.
- Improved communication between auditors and users of accounts.
- Clarification of the liability for fraud.
- Improved control and education of the auditing profession

PII

- The ACCA require that members who hold practising certificates, insolvency licences or investment business certificates must hold Professional Indemnity Insurance (PII) covering all civil liability incurred in connection with the conduct of the firm's business by th partners, directors, or employees.

Arguments in favour of mandatory PII	Arguments against mandatory PII
• Large claims may be made against firms the partners of which may not have the resources to settle such claims. • Firms are at risk from bankruptcy and in the event of such a bankruptcy the whole profession loses credibility.	• Clients and others are encouraged to make claims that, even if ill founded, are often settled out of court. • With PII there is less incentive to fight ill-founded claims.

chapter

7

Audit methodology and approach

In this chapter

- Audit strategy.
- Audit risk and business risk approach.
- Systems audit approach.
- Balance sheet approach.
- Cycle testing.
- Directional testing.

Audit strategy

Exam focus

- This area is critical to your success – selecting an appropriate strategy on a scenario is one of the key skills the examiner is looking for.
- This is likely to be in the form of a scenario based question.

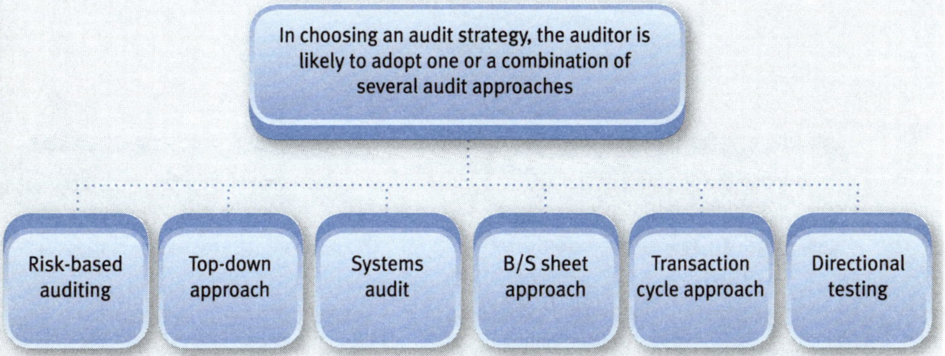
In choosing an audit strategy, the auditor is likely to adopt one or a combination of several audit approaches
Risk-based auditing
Top-down approach
Systems audit
B/S sheet approach
Transaction cycle approach
Directional testing

Audit risk and business risk approach

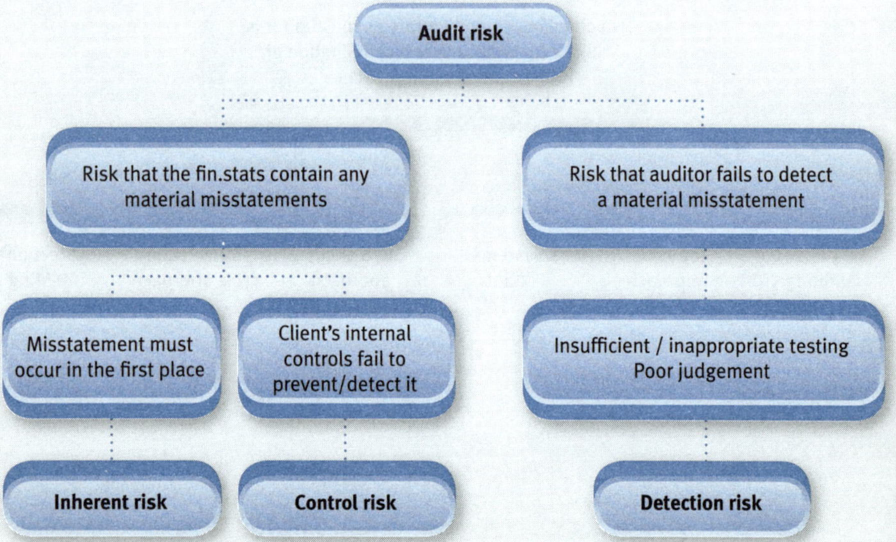

AR = IR x CR x DR

Audit risk approach	
Advantages	**Disadvantages**
• More rational and defensible in court. • More efficient and targeted auditing. • Allows senior staff to evaluate risks allowing delegation of less risky areas. • Approach lends itself to use of audit sampling, IT & CAATs.	• Depends on judgement and subjectivity in assessing IR and CR. • If assessed incorrectly, DR will lead to under or over auditing.

Business risk or 'top down' approach

Business risk approach
• Mirrors increased emphasis on business risk management within businesses. • Enables auditors to assess wider implications of business risks on financial statements e.g do any of the risks have implications for cash flows or the going concern assumptions? Is there any risk of withdrawal of financing? • Enables auditor to add value to a business through the better understanding gained.

Systems audit approach

This requires reliance on systems which prevent/detect errors in the processing of documents into entries in the financial statements.

Particularly relevant for areas where there is a high volume of transactions for example sales, payroll, purchases etc.

Key auditor responsibilities

- **A** Ascertain and document accounting and internal control system
- **C** Consider adequacy of controls
- **C** Compliance test against relevant laws and regulations
- **A** Assess and report findings - are the systems a reliable base from which to prepare accounts?

The balance sheet approach

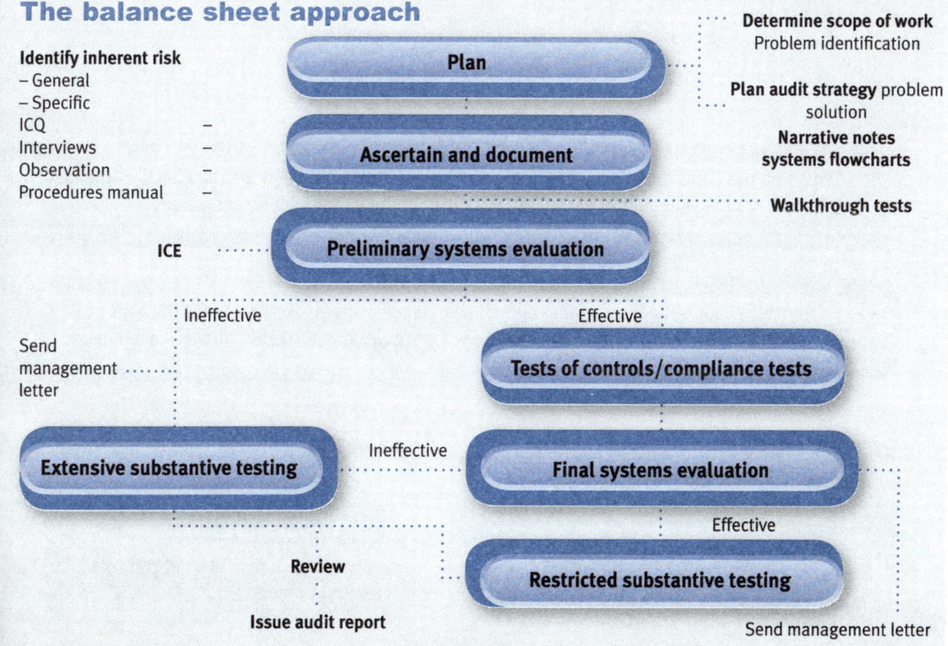

Cycle testing

Balance sheet approach

Works on the basis that profit for the year is the difference between the opening and closing net asset position of the business (excluding shareholder transactions).

Hence by validating the opening and closing balance sheets the profits for the year can be derived – reducing substantially the work required on the profit and loss account.

Advantages

- Appropriate where business and audit risks high
- Substantive approach on balance sheet may be cost-effective
- Appropriate where few transactions

Disadvantages

- May be more costly
- May lead to over-auditing
- Not appropriate if internal controls are unreliable

Cycles testing is a substantive testing technique and differs from systems testing as:

- in systems testing it is the controls which are evaluated and tested
- in cycles testing, it is the individual transactions which are tested to determine whether the information is complete and accurate.

Example: Purchases cycle

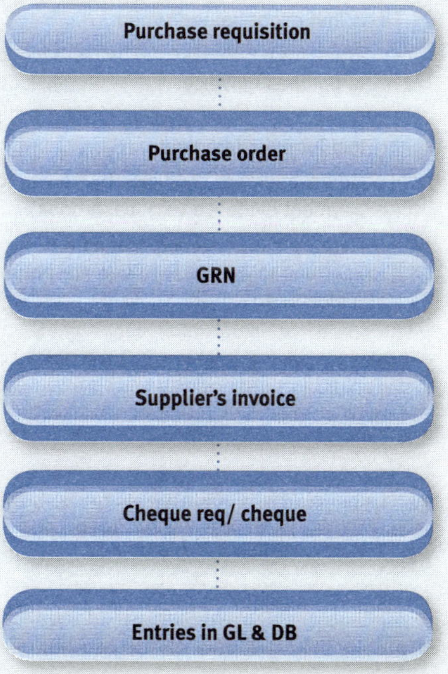

Tests that might be performed:

- Trace from purchases/expense accounts to purchase invoice.
- Inspect supplier's invoice, GRN & PO to test for overstatement.
- Check payment of invoice by tracing to payment evidence (e.g. cash-book).
- Perform cut-off testing around the year end to ensure liabilities are not understated.

Directional testing

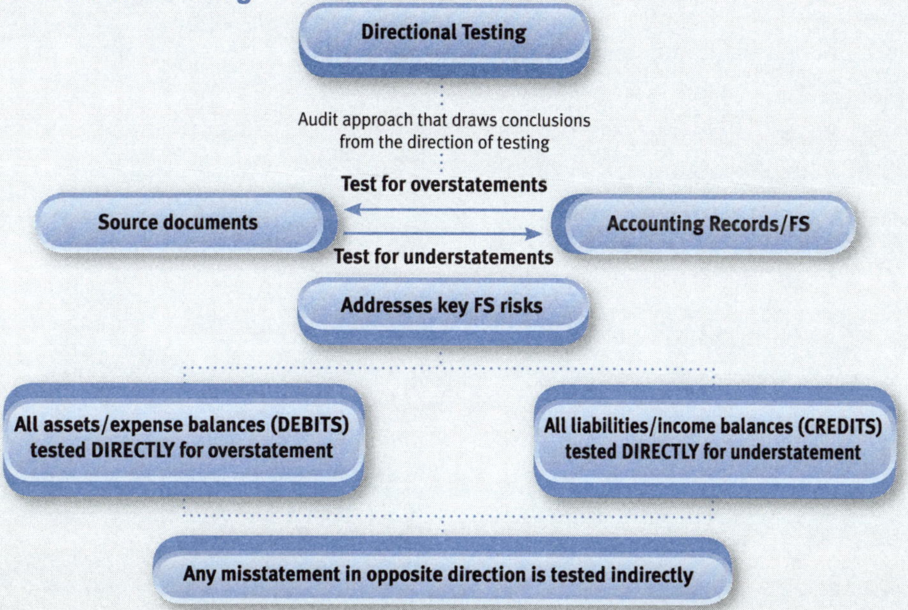

chapter

8

Audit planning

In this chapter

- Audit planning.
- Overall audit plan – audit risk.
- Materiality.
- Risk assessment procedures.
- Assessing the risk of misstatement.
- Computers and the audit process.

Audit planning

Exam focus

Planning is a critical part of the audit process. If it is not carried out with due skill and care, there is a risk that the auditor will be accused of negligence.

In all exams to date there has been one compulsory question involving planning and risk assessment in a range of different scenarios.

At this level, you should be able to:

- consider and determine materiality levels and levels of preliminary risk
- manage the logistics of an audit
- identify critical audit aspects and justify your proposed audit strategy
- demonstrate knowledge of ISAs and good auditing practice.

- Auditors should plan and perform audit with an attitude of professional scepticism.
  - ISA 200 requires auditors to:
  - carry out procedures in compliance with ISAs and ethical guidance (e.g. ACCA rulebook)
  - evaluate overall presentation of the financial statements
  - issue a clear report providing reasonable assurance on the financial statements.

Why plan?

- Establishes audit strategy – the way to achieve audit objectives.
- Ensures appropriate attention devoted to different areas of audit.
- Ensures potential problems identified.
- Facilitates review.
- Ensures reporting deadlines met.
- Minimises client disruption.
- Helps in fee estimation.

Analytical procedures should be used to assist the planning process.

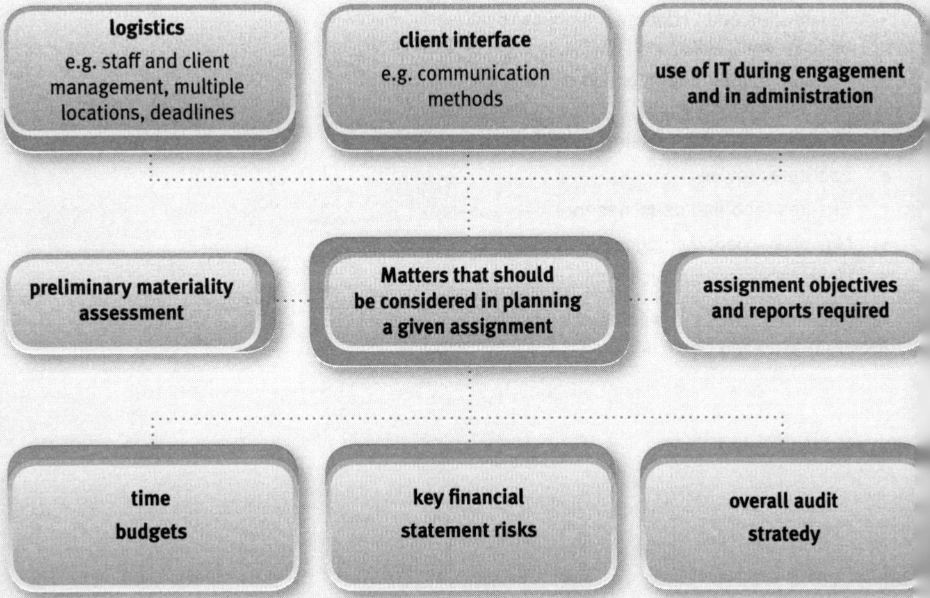
logistics
e.g. staff and client management, multiple locations, deadlines
client interface
e.g. communication methods
use of IT during engagement and in administration
preliminary materiality assessment
Matters that should be considered in planning a given assignment
assignment objectives and reports required
time budgets
key financial statement risks
overall audit stratedy

Overall audit plan – audit risk

ISA 300 - the auditor should document the overall audit strategy (i.e. the general approach) and audit plan (i.e. the detailed procedures to implement the strategy), including any significant changes made during the audit engagement. Should include:

- auditor's understanding of the entity and its environment
- understanding the accounting and internal control systems
- risk and materiality
- the nature, timing and extent of procedures
- the co-ordination, direction, supervision and review.

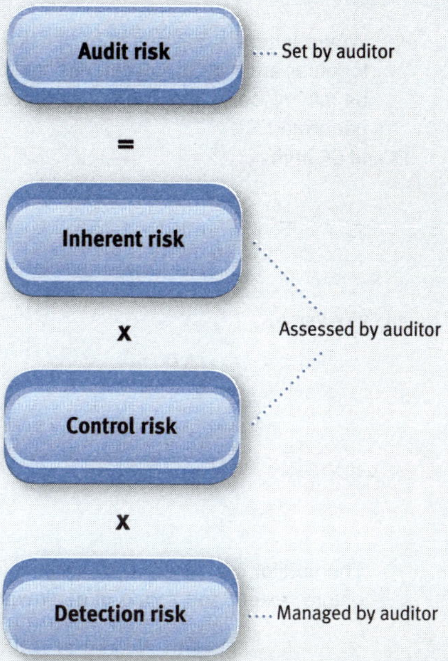

- Where inherent risk and control risk together are high, detection risk must be minimised by the audit procedures performed.

IR and CR high

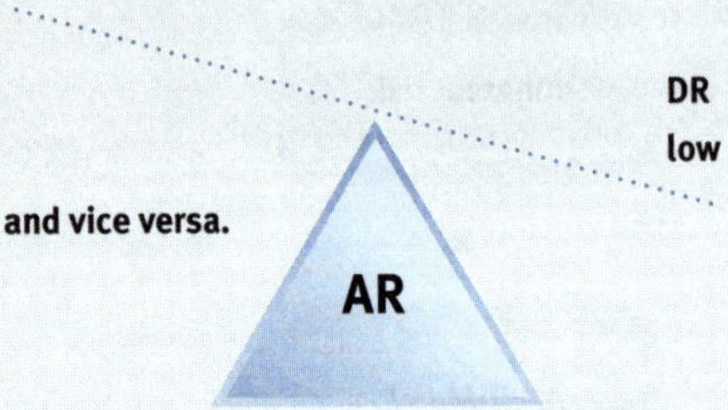

and vice versa.

- The auditor can respond by varying the nature, extent and timing of audit work.

ISA 320 - 'Information is material if its omissions or misstatement could influence the economic decisions of users taken on the basis of the FS'

Materiality should be considered in relation to:

- FS as a whole
- the total of which it would form a part
- the corresponding amount in prior years
- the degree of latitude allowed (e.g. director's remuneration - no latitude)

Ultimately an area of judgement but indicative guidelines are:

Turnover 0.5 - 1%

Pre-tax profits 5 - 10%

Total assets 1 - 2%

Further considerations include:

- Losses or low profits
- Critical points - profits
- Offset and aggregation

Materiality and the audit

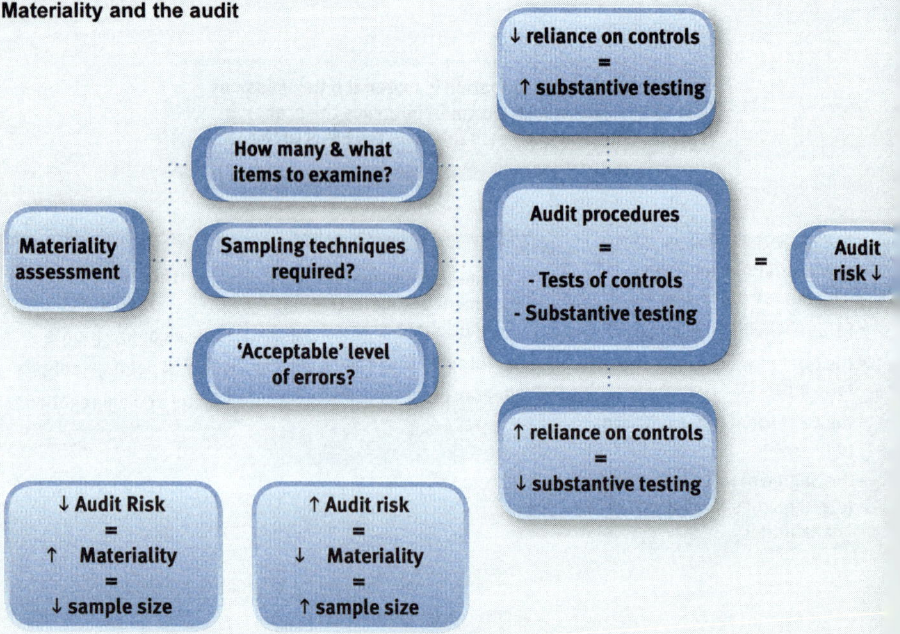

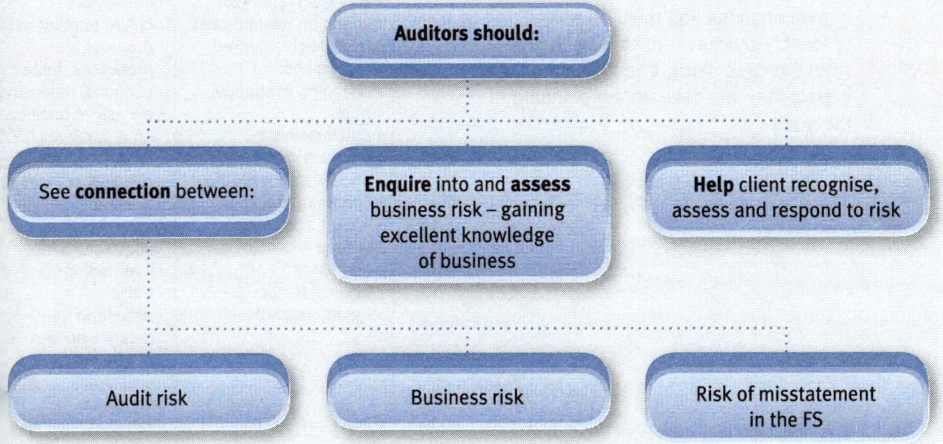
Auditors should:
See **connection** between:
Enquire into and **assess** business risk – gaining excellent knowledge of business
Help client recognise, assess and respond to risk
Audit risk
Business risk
Risk of misstatement in the FS

- Crucial to the business risk approach (see chapter 9) is the identification and analysis of business risks by the auditor.
- In examinations you must be able to identify business risks from the scenario/case study, and indicate what impact they will have on the planning of the audit.

Example 'external risks'	**Example 'internal risks'**
• changing legislation • changing interest rates (N.B. Highly geared companies) • changing exchange rates • public opinion, attitudes, fashions • price wars initiated by competitors • import competition • untried technologies and ideas • political factors. • natural hazards	• employees • failure to modernise products, processes, labour relations, marketing • excessive reliance on a dominant CEO • cash flow difficulties • rapidly increasing gearing • inappropriate acquisitions • overtrading • fraud • excessive reliance on one or few products, customers, suppliers • computer systems failures

Risk assessment procedures

At the planning stage it is important that auditors assess the risks of an audit engagement.

Auditors should

- obtain an understanding of the accounting and internal control systems sufficient to plan the audit and develop an effective audit approach
- use professional judgement to assess the components of audit risk and to design audit procedures to ensure it is reduced to an acceptably low level.

ISA 315

- inquiries of management and others within the entity
- analytical procedures; and
- observation and inspection.

Computers and the audit process

The role of computers in the audit process has already been covered in depth in your previous studies. Here is a reminder of the key areas of consideration:

- The use of computers in carrying out the audit
- CAATs
- Computerised client records
- Considering different types of computer systems and their impact on the audit

chapter

9

Group and transnational audits

In this chapter

- Treatment of groups.
- Group accounts.
- Regulatory requirements of accounting for groups.
- Working with other auditors.
- Special considerations.
- Transnational audits.

Treatment of groups

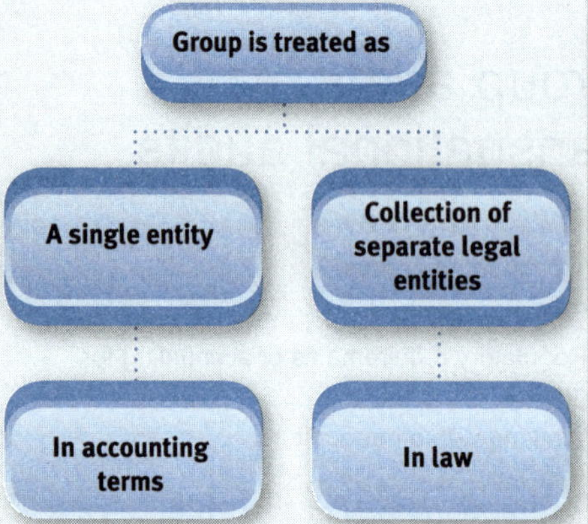

Group accounts

- Group accounts involve consolidation adjustments.
- Relevant IAS must be complied with.
- Subsidiaries may be audited by firms other than holding company auditor.
- Organisation and planning of a group audit is more complex, especially where overseas subsidiaries are involved.

Problems of auditing foreign subsidiary:

- Geographical location.
- Potential for difference in scope than that required in country of parent.
- Different accounting policies may be used.
- Language problems.
- Translation of foreign currency amounts required.

If asked to act as Principal Auditor (where principal auditor will provide audit opinion on whole group regardless of whether they have been involved in the whole group's audit), need to consider appointment based on:

- the materiality of portion of group to be audited by them
- the degree of knowledge regarding the business of the components
- the risk of material errors in the FS of the components audited by other auditors
- the performance of additional procedures on components audited by other auditors.

S 389 CA 85 gives the principal auditor important additional rights to information about subsidiaries. Principal auditors normally send a consolidation questionnaire to each of the subsidiaries auditors requesting information on:

- accounting policies
- accounting details needed for consolidation. Other information relevant for the group FS.

It is the principal auditor's responsibility to review the work of other auditors to satisfy himself that the group accounts give a true and fair view. This is because under S235 CA85 no part of the audit opinion can be delegated by the principal auditor.

Principal auditors review of other auditors work includes:

- review of accounting policies for uniformity
- Consideration of materiality of amounts involved
- considering whether all material areas are covered and whether the work of the other auditors can be relied opon upon, as well as the competence of the other auditors.

Regulatory requirements of accounting for groups

Auditor should ensure investments are properly classified in accordance with their nature and in line with accounting and legal guidelines – as subsidiaries, associates, JVs and other investments. Main areas of consideration are:

- **Accounting policies** if not uniform then consolidation adjustments required
- Inter-company transaction and items in transit will require consolidation adjustments
- Sch 4CA 85/89 Accounting periods should be co-terminus (or within three months of each other). Otherwise consolidation adjustments required
- Need to consider changes in group composition and the requirements in FRS2 for acquisition accounting
- Consideratio of loss-makin subsidiaries and whether there is a nee to write-dowr an investmen or whether there is goodw impairment

- **Contingencies** eg inter-company guaranteed loans should be disclosed per FRS 12
- **Subsequent events** need to consider whether there have been any additions or disposals
- Where there are restrictior on distributions of profit, the should be indicated in the F

Working with other auditors

Joint audits arise when the parent company auditors are appointed jointly with the existing auditors of a subsidiary

Advantages:	Disadvantages:
• Improved service through firms different expertise • Improved geographical coverage Use of two independent firms can provide added assurance to client	• Each joint auditor takes responsibility for the other's shortcomings • May be more expensive • Different firm's audit methods may not be reconciled • Close control of division of work is required

Requirements for effective joint audits:

- Preliminary planning meeting between the two firms to decide on timing, work allocation etc.
- Final meeting to discuss audit issues, conclusions, management letter and joint audit opinion.
- Proper work allocation to avoid dominance.
- Both firms should have adequate professional indemnity insurance.

Special considerations

Subsidiaries in developing countries may not have a fully developed system of accounting and auditing standards. Hence, group auditor can:

- request group directors to adjust FS to comply with Uk standards
- require the local auditor to conform to ISAs or to perform further audit procedures.

If one or more of subsidiaries has a modified audit report (regardless of who the auditor was), principal auditor should:

- ignore the matter if immaterial at a group level
- modify the group audit opinion if material at a group level
- no mention is made of Other Auditor.

In accounting terms (FRS 2), group is a single entity. In legal terms, however, it is a collection of legal entities - which may mean that a component entity may not be a going concern without the support of the group.

The custom is for the directors to give the auditor a comfort/support letter assuring tha the group will support the subsidiary - this will be taken by the auditor as valid audit evidence of the going concern basis of the subsidiaries FS.

Exam focus

- At this level, scenarios will likely include a complex element which may involve groups. As such, it is important to be aware of the main accounting and auditing issues involved.
- Accounting standards in this area include: FRS 2 Accounting for Subsidia Undertaking, FRS 6 Acquisitions

and Mergers, FRS 7 Fair Values in Acquisition Accounting, FRS 9 Associates and Joint Ventures, FRS 10 Goodwill and Intangible Assets.

Transnational audits

Definition

Transnational audit means an audit of financial statements which are or may be relied upon outside the audited entity's home jurisdiction.

- Reliance on these audits might be for purposes of significant lending, investment or regulatory decisions.
- Audits will include those of financial statements of all companies with listed equity or debt and other public interest entities which attract particular public attention because of their size, products or services provided.

Who monitors them?
Transnational Audit Committee (TAC)

How do they differ?
- Listing requirements
- Corporate governance requirements
- Applicable accounting and auditing standards

Globalisation

- Goods, services, capital and even people move more easily across national borders than ever before.
- Global businesses operate in widely different legal and ethical systems.
- As a result audit firms have to have the resources and expertise to operate in every country and have to know how to audit highly regulated modern businesses.

- Only the large audit firms can acquire the global expertise to handle such audits.

Advantages	Disadvantages
• Wide ranging expertise • Global facilities • Can invest in expensive systems and necessary IT to meet needs of international clients	• Lack of competition and choice, particularly for large companies

The concentration of the audit market into a few very large firms has come about because of the growth of globalisation in world markets everywhere.

- The larger firms found that **amalgamations** amongst the audit firms were the way forward and as a result the world audit market is now concentrated in very few firms.
- **Affiliation** is used by the larger accounting firms to develop an internationally recognised brand name.
- **Co-operation** is used by the mid-tier firms who join an international co-operative of firms who send each other business, but retain their own trading name in their home countries.

chapter

10

Evidence

In this chapter

- Obtaining audit evidence.
- Documentation.
- Related party transactions.
- Management representations.
- Using the work of an expert.

Obtaining audit evidence

ISA 500 audit evidence, states that ' auditors should obtain SUFFICIENT APPROPRIATE audit evidence to be able to draw reasonable conclusions on which to base the audit opinion'

Sufficient - the necessary quantity must be obtained

Appropriate - the audit evidence must be of a necessary quality - both relevant and reliable

SUFFICIENCY - as determined by a no. of factors e.g. Materiality of item being examined, auditor's knowledge and judgement (CAKE - cumulatively acquired audit knowledge and experience)

Relevant - Evidence is required that will enable auditor to draw conclusions on the financial statement assertions

Reliable - auditor should consider source and its reliability - e.g. written evidence more reliable than oral evidence

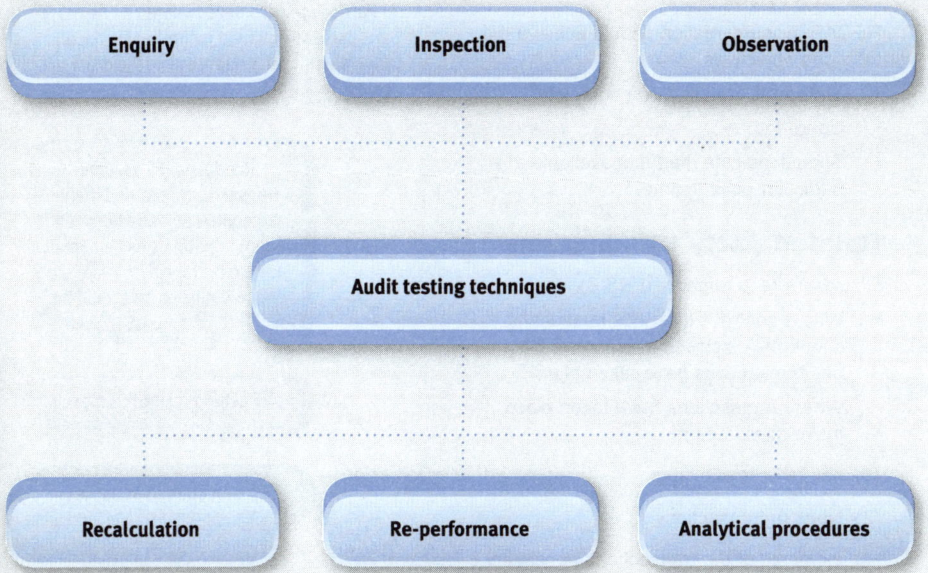
Enquiry
Inspection
Observation
Audit testing techniques
Recalculation
Re-performance
Analytical procedures

Documentation

RECAP: Documentation should achieve the following objectives.

- Sufficiently detailed and complete
- Up-to-date
- Should indicate the facts available at a particular point in time.

Related party transactions

Disclosure requirements (FRS 8):

- Where control exists, this relationship should be disclosed irrespective whether any transactions have taken place
- Where transactions have taken place, make disclosure of:

(1) nature of relationship

(2) types of transactions

(3) elements of the transactions necessary for an understanding of the FS.

Parties are considered related if one party has the ability to control or exercise significant influence over the other

Readers of FS assume transactions recorded in the accounts are made between independent parties and are at arm's length - where there are 'related parties' this must be disclosed

Deemed related parties

Presumed related parties

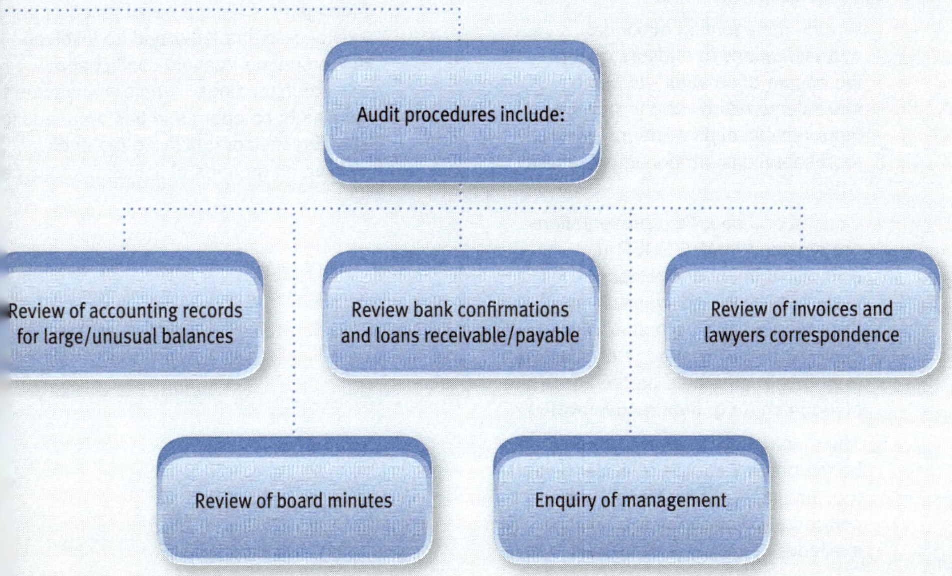
Audit procedures include:
Review of accounting records for large/unusual balances
Review bank confirmations and loans receivable/payable
Review of invoices and lawyers correspondence
Review of board minutes
Enquiry of management

Management representations

Key revision points

- Where management make oral representations to auditors during the course of an audit - to avoid misunderstandings and to provide more reliable audit evidence, these representations are documented in a letter.
- General and specific representations are provided - e.g. GENERAL: acknowledgment of directors responsibility for the preparation of FS and SPECIFIC: a matter which is confined to the knowledge of directors (e.g. details of related parties) or is one of judgment (e.g. debt recoverability).
- The management representations may be the primary source of evidence but they are NOT a substitute for other corroborative evidence that may be available.
- If contradictory evidence is found, further investigation is required.
- Management should be informed of the existence of the letter and be involved in the drafting to avoid conflict and misunderstandings - where management refuses to co-operate in this area, auditors should consider qualifying the audit opinion on grounds of limitation of scope

Using the work of an expert

EXPERT = Person/Firm providing special skill, knowledge and experience other than auditing

Auditors need to obtain **sufficient appropriate** evidence that the work performed by expert is adequate for audit purposes

Needs to assess **objectivity** and **professional competence** of the expert

1. Expert evidence should be requested by client

2. Scope of work must be pre-agreed between auditor, client and expert

3. Auditors must evaluate findings of expert (e.g. review assumptions....)

4. Auditor must consider implications for audit report where...
   - Client refuses to appoint expert or reappoint another for second opinion
   - Where relevance and reliability of expert evidence is uncertain
   - Client refuses to allow use of expert evidence

Exam focus

- The syllabus area on audit evidence is critical to the exam. A common exam question in the past has been scenario based with the requirement to "state the audit evidence you would expect to find".
- You will be expected to be aware of the relative merits of different types of evidence and how far they are reliable. You will also be expected to consider alternative sources.
- The key points covered by the ISAs in this section will provide you with the tools to approach such a question – you will, however, need to apply your knowledge as far as possible to the scenario given!

chapter

11

Completion

In this chapter

- Overall review of financial statements.
- Opening balances & comparatives.
- Unaudited published information.
- Events after the balance sheet date.
- Going concern.

Overall review of the financial statements

Overall review of financial statements

- **Statutory requirements & accounting standards**
- **Presentation & disclosure**
- **Consistency**

Opening balances and comparatives

ISA 510 Opening Balances

New auditor will need to satisfy self of opening position

- Consult management
- Review records, accounts and control procedures in previous periods
- Consult with previous auditor
- Perform audit procedures
- Consider implications for report if dissatisfied still

Continuing auditor will need to ensure

- Amounts correctly brought forward
- Corresponding amounts correctly classified and disclosed
- Accounting policies consistently applied

ISA 710 Comparatives

Sufficient appropriate evidence is required to ensure:

- Accounting policies used for comparatives are consistent with those of current period and disclosures made where this is not the case
- Comparatives agree with prior audited FS
- Where comparatives adjusted/ restated as required by legislation/ accounting standards, appropriate disclosures made.

Unaudited published information

Although auditors express an opinion on the audited FS only, they need to consider whether the Other Information (often disclosed alongside the FS) contains misstatements or inconsistencies.

In a serious situation, the auditor could also use his rights under s387 CABS to be heard at any general meting or any business of the meeting which concerns him as auditor.

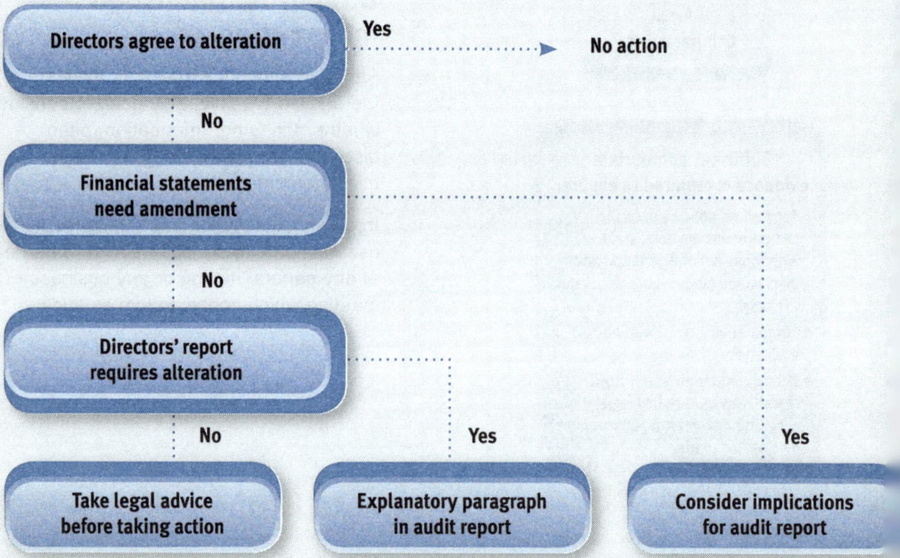
Directors agree to alteration
Yes
No action
No
Financial statements need amendment
No
Directors' report requires alteration
No
Yes
Yes
Take legal advice before taking action
Explanatory paragraph in audit report
Consider implications for audit report

Events after the balance sheet date

Up to the date of the audit report

Auditors should peform procedures **designed to obtain sufficient appropriate audit evidence that all events up** to the date of the auditor's report that may require adjustment or disclosure have been identified.

After the date of the audit report but before the FS are issued

Auditor **has no responsibility** to perform procedures or make enquiry regarding FS after audit report date. If auditor becomes aware of amendment should discuss with management and consider implications for audit report.

After the FS are issued

Auditor has **no obligation** to make any inquiry regarding FS. If new information relating to prior to the date of auditor's report comes to light, auditor should consider revision of FS and discuss with management.

FRs 21 (SSAP 17) provides guidance in this area of adjusting and non-adjusting events

Non-adjusting (arises after BS date and concerns conditions non-existent at BS date) requires disclosure only: eg Destruction of significant asset, issues of shares

Adjusting (provides additional evidence of conditions existing at the BS date) requires adjustment to the FS and notes: eg insolvency of receivable after BS date, or going concern problem

Going concern

Fundamental principle: When **planning** and performing auditing procedures and in **evaluating** the results, the auditor should consider the appropriateness of **management's** use of the going concern assumption in the preparation of the FS.

Management is required to make an assessment of the enterprise's ability to continue for the foreseeable future considering the following factors:

Financial eg

- BS position
- Budgeted negative cash flows
- Maturing debts without realistic prospect of repayment

Operating eg

- Loss of key management without replacement
- Loss of major market

Other eg

- Non-compliance with capital or other statutory requirements

Auditors must review management's going concern assessment, gather sufficient appropriate evidence to confirm/dispel whether a material uncertainty exists and seek management representations regarding future plans. In carrying out evaluation, procedures should include:

* Analysing and discussing latest and budgeted financial information
* Reading board minutes for reference to financial difficulties and future plans
* Review loan agreement terms and determining whether there has been or will likely by any breach

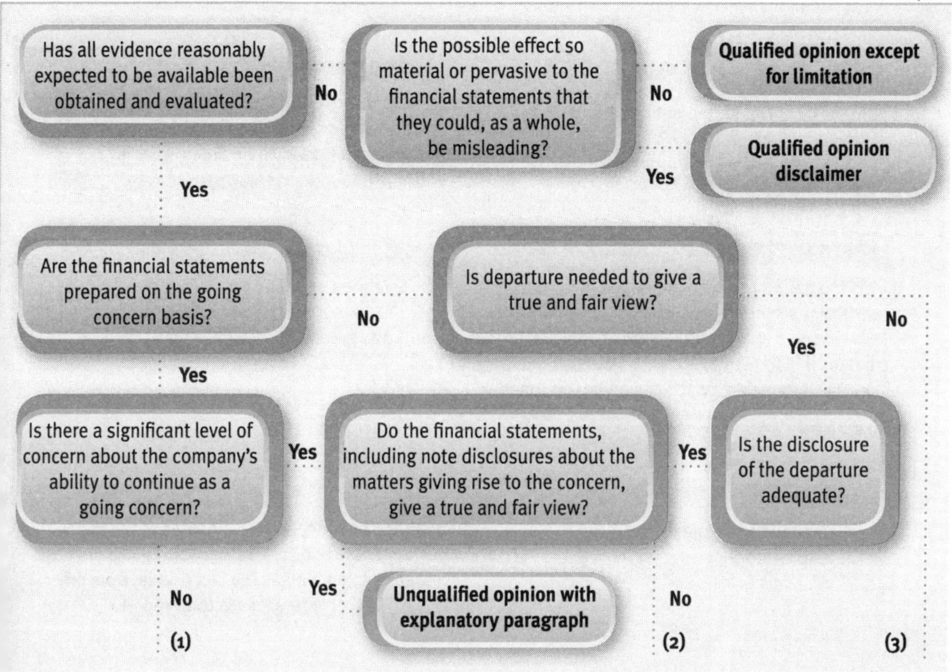
Has all evidence reasonably expected to be available been obtained and evaluated?
No
Is the possible effect so material or pervasive to the financial statements that they could, as a whole, be misleading?
No
Qualified opinion except for limitation
Yes
Qualified opinion disclaimer
Yes
Are the financial statements prepared on the going concern basis?
No
Is departure needed to give a true and fair view?
Yes
No
Yes
Is there a significant level of concern about the company's ability to continue as a going concern?
Yes
Do the financial statements, including note disclosures about the matters giving rise to the concern, give a true and fair view?
Yes
Is the disclosure of the departure adequate?
No
(1)
Yes
Unqualified opinion with explanatory paragraph
No
(2)
(3)

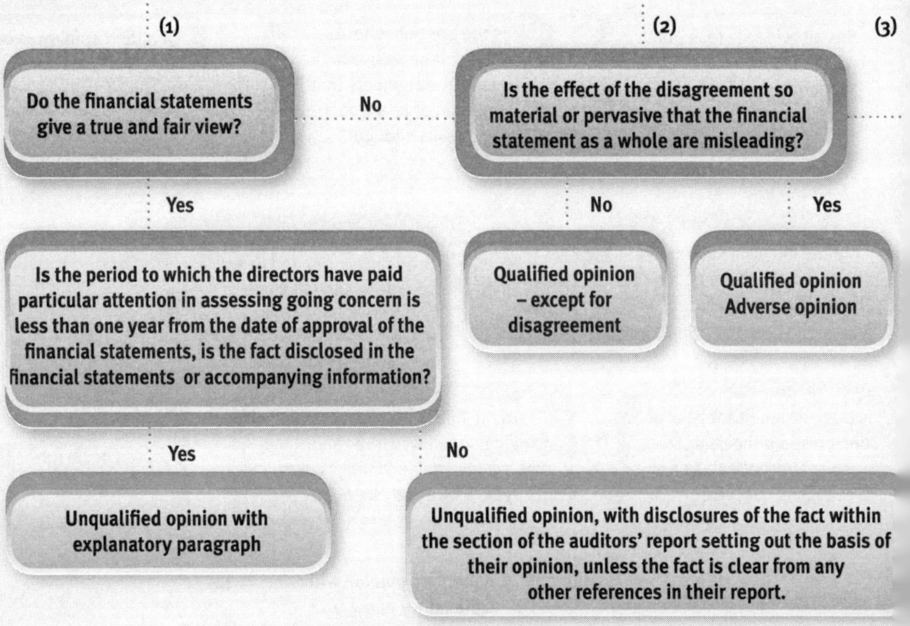
(1)
Do the financial statements give a true and fair view?
No
(2)
Is the effect of the disagreement so material or pervasive that the financial statement as a whole are misleading?
(3)
Yes
Is the period to which the directors have paid particular attention in assessing going concern is less than one year from the date of approval of the financial statements, is the fact disclosed in the financial statements or accompanying information?
No
Qualified opinion – except for disagreement
Yes
Qualified opinion Adverse opinion
Yes
Unqualified opinion with explanatory paragraph
No
Unqualified opinion, with disclosures of the fact within the section of the auditors' report setting out the basis of their opinion, unless the fact is clear from any other references in their report.

Exam focus

- Together with the planning stage, the review stage is one of the critical processes in the audit. Analytical procedures will be key here!
- The auditor will need to exercise skill and judgment to evaluate the evidence obtained and the way forward: Is the entity a going concern? Are additional procedures required or should we move directly to the formation of audit opinion?
- Be prepared to be asked to form such a judgment!

chapter

12

Audit-related services

In this chapter

- Definitions.
- Types of engagement.
- Engagements to compile financial information.
- Engagements to perform agreed-upon procedures.
- Engagements to review financial information.

Definitions

Definition

Attest engagement: to attest to something is to bear witness or affirm it.

Due diligence: a term to describe a wide range of services performed by professional accountants with or without the expression of a professional opinion. Often found in connection with mergers and acquisitions - e.g. to ensure that assets and liabilities are as stated

Direct reporting: engagements where accountants are required to give a special report (with an opinion) on some aspects of a client's affairs to a third party at the request of the client in accordance with instructions (e.g. for tax purposes).

Agreed-upon procedures: an engagement where the procedures to be performed by the professional accountant are predetermined. The professional accountant provides a report with the factual findings but no opinion is provided.

Compilation reports: this is not an audit and no assurance/opinion is provided. It is an engagement where information/data is compiled in accordance with the client's instructions.

Engagements to review financial information: similar to audit, but procedures are less detailed. Provides only a LIMITED level of assurance that the information is free from financial misstatement as expressed in the form of negative assurance.

Types of engagement

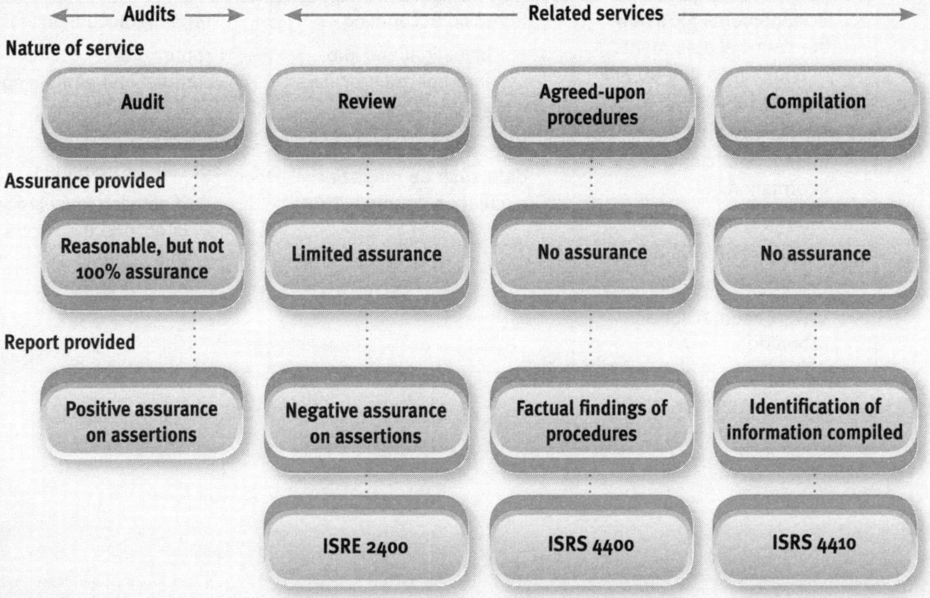

Reviews	Agreed-upon procedures	Compilations
• Engagements to review the financial statements of companies that do not have to be audited (eg, small companies). • Interim financial information. • 'Due diligence' assignments. • PFI engagements. • Environmental/social reporting	• Forensic accounting – investigations into fraud or malpractice. • Verifying insurance claims. • Reporting on non-financial data such as magazine circulation figures.	• Preparing accounts. • Preparing tax computations and acting as an agent for tax matters. • Special tax enquiries – a detailed knowledge is outside the scope of this syllabus.

Engagements to compile financial information

Auditors may sometimes be engaged to report on financial information other than FS - per ISA 800 e.g. statement of cash receipts and disbursements and a report on the FS prepared on the entity's income tax purposes.

If auditors are asked to provide opinion on summarised FS, then they may NOT do this unless they have already expressed an audit opinion on the full FS.

All such engagements should be preceded by an engagement letter and followed by a report detailing the intended user the work carried out, the results and the opinion formed.

Where the accountant is asked to compile financial information, he is NOT conducting an audit and not expressing any assurance. This should be made clear in the report and the accountant should take care to comply with the IFAC Code.

ISRS 4410 governs work in this area - and requirements are as follows.

- Terms of engagement are defined.
- Planning and documentation.
- Obtaining knowledge of the business and its operations.
- Management's responsibility.
- Measures to address unsatisfactory information provided by client.
- Form of report - ensure it is stated that no audit/review work has been performed.

Engagements to perform agreed-upon procedures

Auditor provides report on factual findings and no assurance is expressed (e.g. reports on insurance claims, reports on compliance with industry regulations).

Users assess for themselves the procedures undertaken and results and draw their own conclusions.

Engagement letter is paramount to outline purpose and nature of assignment and form of report.

Final report must also include the intended users and that distribution is limited and subject to the auditors consent.

Engagements to review financial statements

This engagement falls short of a full audit bu still provides some assurance in the form of a negative assurance opinion.

In conducting these reviews, auditors should plan and perform them with an attitude of professional scepticism recognising that circumstances may exist that cause the FS to be materially misstated. Auditors should obtain sufficient appropriate audit evidence, mainly in the form of analytical procedures.

Other procedures include:

- obtaining an understanding of the business and its key risks
- inquiries regarding all the material FS assertions
- inquiries regarding actions taken at meetings of shareholders and directors

- obtaining and reading other auditors reports
- obtaining written representations from management where appropriate
- subsequent events testing.

Although there is currently no requirement for the audit of interim financial Information - where management request an audit, the review work required so as to provide negative assurance is similar to that described above.

Exam focus

- More recently, investors and other company stakeholders have found a need for other services and other types of assurance – as such, it is important to be aware of the guidelines in this area and the assurance levels (if any) to be provided in each case.
- Audit-related services and assurance services are areas that have been examined in the past, both as part of scenarios and directly as discussion questions.

chapter 13

Assurance services

In this chapter

- Assurance engagements.
- Systems reliability.
- Value for money.
- E-commerce.
- Environmental impact on FS.
- Environmental audits and reporting.
- Social matters.

Assurance engagements

Definition

An **assurance engagement** is an engagement in which a practitioner expresses a conclusion designed to enhance the degree of confidence of the intended users other than the responsible party about the outcome of evaluating a subject matter against criteria.

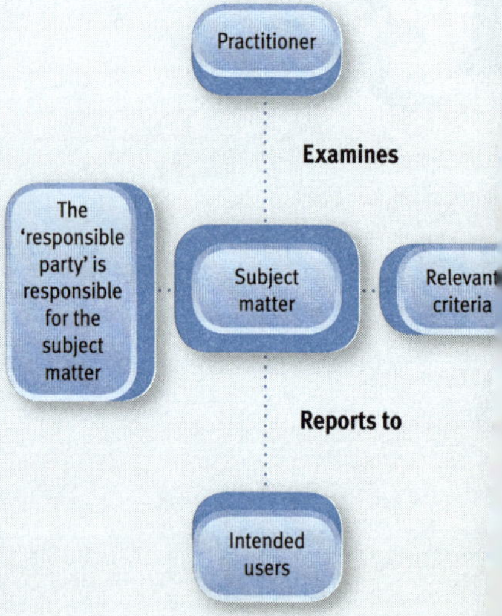

The two types of assurance engagement

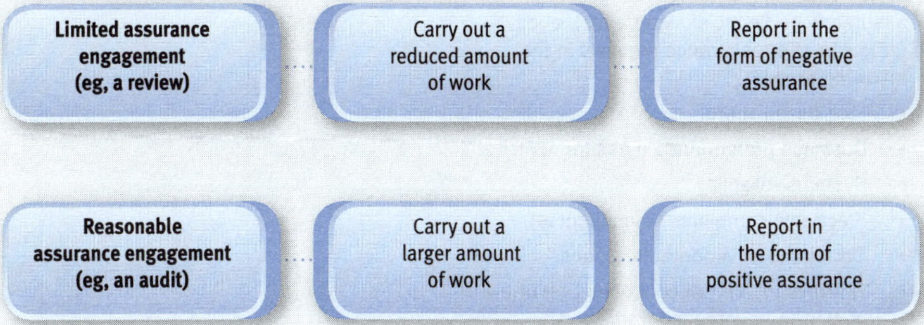

As well as the traditional audit (offering reasonable assurance on financial statements) and review (offering limited assurance on financial statements), audit firms can offer assurance services in the following areas.

- Risk assessment.
- Business performance measurement.
- Systems reliability.
- Electronic commerce (e-commerce).
- Social and environmental issues.
- Reviews of internal control as part of the corporate governance framework.
- Best value/value for money work in private/public sector organisations.
- Ethical supply chain management.

Systems reliability

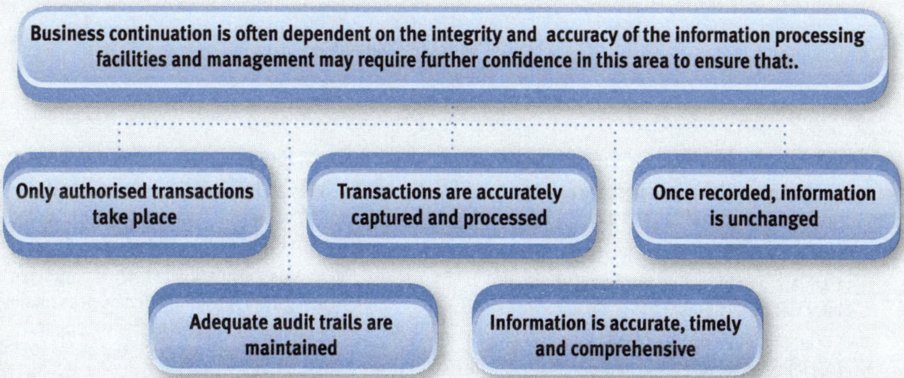

Procedures include:

- assess the control environment
- assess business and audit risks
- assess effectiveness of control policies and procedures
- assess the methods and records established to identify, assemble, analyse, calculate and report transactions
- Ttest transactions (use CAATs where applicable).

Value for money

Performance measurement value for money

Assurance is often sought to provide benefits such as:

- Motivational impetus on managers
- Evaluation of branch performance and information systems
- Evaluation of Economy, Effectiveness and Efficiency of service provision

VFM audits usually carried out in the public sector as this information is of great relevance to the public whose funds are used!

VFM is usually defined in terms of the 3Es Efficiency, Economy and Effectiveness and in which government departments cooperate to achieve the 3 Es.

Financial and non-financial criteria are important for the ratios and key performance indicators such as average costs for specific treatments in hospitals, repeat purchases by customers in the retail sector.

E-commerce

Technology is used in three main ways:

E-commerce - business is conducted over the internet rather than by paper methods.

Electronic Data Interchange (EDI) - standard method of transmitting documents (e.g. invoices, orders) rather than by hard copy.

Secure Electronic Transmission (SET) - an extension of EDI for the settlement of payments (mainly credit cards).

Risks include:

- exposure to competitors
- acts of malice
- money laundering
- loss of earnings
- corruption of financial data
- theft of intellectual property.

Risk management procedures include:

- risk assessment in essential
- internal audit is of greater importance
- maintaining systems access control (e.g. passwords and physical security)
- frequent backups
- maintaining electronic audit trails (and hard copies).

E-commerce provides a number of challenges to the auditor, which need to be considered prior to accepting/continuing with an audit client and during the planning process.

- Need for technical expertise.
- Increased audit risk.
- Going concern issue more problematic.
- Some parts of the system may be outsourced.

- Focus of existent controls may not cover storage and recording of transactions but execution.
- If auditors have assisted in the establishment of the system this is a conflict of interest.
- In the early stages of e-commerce, auditor may not be able to rely on analytical procedures.

Environmental impact on FS

Companies may or may not have to address environmental matters where they are relevant, the risks of material misstatement in the FS are:

- Provisions e.g. site restoration costs
- Contingent Liabilities (eg pending legislation)
- Asset values (non current assets or inventories may be affected)
- Accounting for capital/revenue expenditure to meet costs compliance
- Product redesign costs

Going concern/Product viability considerations

The auditor is required to obtain knowledge which is sufficient to enable him to identify and understand the events/transactions/ practices that may have a significant effect on the audit of the FS

- FRS 12 Provisions, Contingent Liabilities and Fixed Assets
- FRS 11 Impairment of Gixed Assets and Goodwill

Measuring the effects of environmental matters is problematic:

- Possible timelag between event occurring and being identified
- Accounting estimates subject to assumptions
- Environmental laws evolving and subject to interpretation
- Liabilities arising from legal, constructive obligations but also perhaps from 'perceived' moral obligations

Appropriate audit procedures include:

- Incorporate environmental concerns in planning procedures
- Enquire of management as to any systems or controls in place to identify risk, evaluate control and account for environmental matters
- Obtain written representations form management on environmental matters
- Review board minutes
- Include environmental matters in review of appropriateness of going concern.

Environmental audits and reporting

Environmental audit: a management tool (or regulatory agency tool) comprising a systematic, documented, periodic and objective evaluation of how well organizations, management and equipment are performing with the aim of contributing to safeguarding the environment by facilitating management control of environmental practices, and assessing compliance with company policies, which would include meeting regulatory requirements and standards applicable.

Eco-audit scheme voluntary EU environmental auditing scheme established for industrial companies

It is recommended that the **Annual Report** contains:

- The company's environmental policy
- The impact of business on environment

More Specific matters reported:

- Sustainability
- Targets achieved
- Compliance with regulations
- Emissions
- Industrial legacies
- ISO 14001

Note: Report also contains:

- Methodology used
- Opinion

Social matters

Many companies now publish social and environmental reports but few attach audit reports to these reports. It is possible:

- To conduct an audit on social, environmental or H&S issues, and/or
- To attest to the report to add assurance

Social matters include:

Ethical matters, Charitable donations, Employment policies, Training policies, Human rights, Health and Safety

Exam focus

- Corporate social responsibility and the associated reporting of environmental and social matters continues to be a hot topic in the business world, and could therefore form the basis of an interesting exam question.
- It is important to consider both the accounting and reporting implications when dealing with a company's environmental position.

chapter 14

Prospective financial information

In this chapter

- PFI.
- Assurance procedures.

Prospective financial information

A reporting accountant may be asked to provide an opinion on prospective (future) financial information in the form of a forecast and/or projection (ISAE 3400 is the authoritative standard in this area).

The APB has issued four Statements of Investment Circular Reporting Standards (SIR's). SIR 3000 and SIR 4000 provide guidance specific to profit forecasts and pro-forma financial information respectively

PFI = Financial information based on assumptions about events that may occur in the future and possible actions by the entity.

FORECAST= PFI based on management expectations (best-estimate assumptions).

PROJECTION= PFI based on hypothetical assumptions about future events that may or may not take place or based on a combination of best-estimate and hypothetical assumptions.

Prior to **ACCEPTANCE** of a PFI engagement, the auditor must consider:

- The intended users
- Whether the information will be for general or limited distribution
- The nature of assumptions: best estimate or hypothetical?
- Elements to be included and period covered

Assurance procedures

Agree letter of engagement and form of opinion: Negative assurance, Management responsibility for preparation of forecast, restriction on distribution

Have all cost implications been accounted for in the use of hypothetical assumptions (e.g. staff required, prospective capacity)?

Obtain management representations on the intended use of the PFI, management's responsibility for the preparation of PFI, and the completeness of significant assumptions.

Typical procedures include:

Obtain sufficient knowledge of business

Assess source and reliability of management's best-estimate assumptions - Are they reliable and realistic?

Are forecasts and supporting schedules arithmetically correct? Are they consistent with management's plan? How do they compare to results to date?

Exam focus

This is an area that has been examined in the past and is of importance where intended users will rely on the opinion on PFI.

chapter

15

Forensic audits

In this chapter

- Forensic accounting.
- Applications.
- Process.

Forensic accounting

Definition

Forensic accounting is a specialist branch of the profession carried out by forensic accountants and encompassing forensic auditing and investigation.

Applications of forensic accounting

Application	Examples	Type of work performed
Fraud investigations	Employee embezzlement of company funds, tax evasion, insider dealing.	Funds tracing, asset identification and recovery, forensic intelligence gathering, due diligence reviews, interviews, detailed review of documentary evidence.
Insurance claims	Business interruptions, property losses, motor vehicle incidents, personal liability claims, cases of medical malpractice, wrongful dismissal.	Detailed review of the policy from either an insured or insurer's perspective to investigate coverage issues, identification of appropriate method of calculating the loss, quantification of losses
Professional negligence	Loss suffered as a result of placing reliance on professional adviser	Advising on merits of a case in regards to liability, quantifying losses.
Shareholder, partnership and matrimonial disputes	Determination of funds to be included in settlements, as benefits or distributions	Detailed analysis of numerous years accounting records to quantify the issues in dispute, tracing, locating and evaluation of assets

Process

Investigative procedures

- Locate documents, economic information, assets, a person or company
- Identify an expert witness
- Gather proof of occurrence of an event
- Carry out interviews
- Carry out detailed review of documentary evidence
- Perform due diligence review

Evidence →

Evaluation

- Calculate economic damages
- Perform regression or sensitivity analyses
- Summarise large numbers of transactions
- Perform present value calculations
- Utilise computerised applications to analyse data
- Use charts and graphs to explain analysis

Exam focus

- A question on forensic auditing would allow many areas of knowledge to be tested outside of the 'standard' audit scenario.
- The pilot paper contains a question on forensic auditing.
- Approach any question on forensic auditing with an open mind, consider what the question is asking for and address the requirements – **do not** automatically assume it is related to finding or investigating a fraud!

chapter 16

Internal audit

In this chapter

- Internal audit.
- Operational and compliance audits.
- Outsourcing internal audit.

Internal audit

Internal audit is an appraisal activity established by management for the review of the accounting and internal control systems as a service to the entity. It reviews, monitors and makes recommendations for the improvements of systems.

Other activities include:

- examination and evaluation of financial and operating information
- VFM audits
- review of compliance with external laws and regulations
- review of internal policies
- review of the authorisation of transactions
- special investigations (e.g. into fraud)
- risk assessments.

Differences between external and internal auditors

	Internal auditor	External auditor
Objectives	Report to management assist in managing and running business	Report to S/Hs T+F CA85 Credibility of FS
Legal basis	Not required except finance service companies Strongly recommended for PLCs - Turnbull	CA85 All companes except small private companies
Scope	As dictated by management	Statute and as requested by management
Approach to work	Risk-based Reflecting technique used by EAs	Risk based As per ISAs/PN bulletins
Responsibility	To management	To shareholder

Operational and compliance audits

Two of the main types of work undertaken by an internal audit department can be categorised as operational or compliance audits.

	Operational	**Compliance**
Main focus	Effectiveness, operation and adherence of business to **internal** controls.	Compliance of business with **external** laws, rules and regulations.
Risk addressed	Failure of internal controls could lead to financial loss, operational inefficiency, etc.	Compliance failures could result in criminal penalties, fines and costs, executive time in defending actions, legal fees, investigations, bad publicity, etc.
Other areas of review	Ways to improve operational economy, efficiency and effectiveness.	• Appropriateness of, and adherence with, internal processes and procedures supporting compliance. • Maintenance of documentation supporting compliance. • Management responsibilities.

- Although the objectives of internal and external audit differ, the objectives are often similar.
- External auditors must obtain a sufficient understanding of the IA function to assist in the planning and developing of an effective audit approach and to determine whether it is possible to rely on IA work.

Factors to consider include:

- The organisational status of IA
- The scope of the IA function
- The technical competence of the IAs
- Due professional care

Outsourcing IA

A fairly recent development in client services is the outsourcing of IA by companies to a professional firm.

Advantages	Disadvantages
• More independence than in-house department • Higher quality • More flexibility • Expert training • Professional firm has ethical standards can be sued and has insurance • More cost effective	• Lack of intimate knowledge of business and employees • Not directly under control of company • Professional fees tend to be high

chapter

17

Outsourcing

In this chapter

- Reasons for outsourcing.
- Pros & cons.
- Outsourcing and the auditor.

Reasons for outsourcing

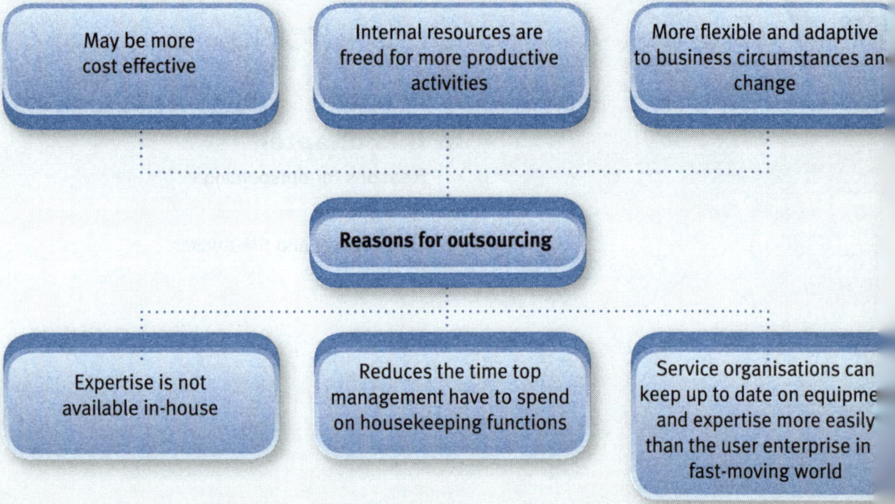

Pros and cons

Outsourcing Pros & cons

Advantages

- Quality of service provided.
- Market value for services.
- Overcoming a skill shortage.
- No waste.
- Risk transfer.
- Disposal of a non-core activity
- Flexibility to deal with peaks and troughs in workload
- Maintenance of technical knowledge (e.g. Tax rules)
- Ability to change supplier if dissatisfied

Drawbacks

- No guarantee of quality.
- The captive customer syndrome.
- Conflicts of interest.
- Impact on morale.
- Cost control.
- Some loss of control.

Outsourcing and the auditor

Outsourcing is developing further as companies are looking to outsource services for cost effectiveness, quality, etc (eg data processing, pensions, information technology, due diligence work, tax management, custody of assets).

Outsourcing and the auditor:
The auditors should identify whether the client uses service organizations for outsourcing and assess the effect of such use on the procedures necessary to obtain sufficient appropriate audit evidence to determine whether the FS show a true and fair view. The following points should be considered .

Insourcing is the opposite to outsourcing where a business has developed a specialism for an aspect of its own business and also provides that service to others.

Consider quality and location of audit evidence – is the evidence held at client adequate?

During 'planning', to determine which activities are out sourced.

Impact on inherent risk, control risk and the clients control environment.

When relying on a report issuec by the auditors of the service organization, the client's audito should consider the scope of the work performed and if it is sufficient and appropriate for it intended use.

Knowledge as to the contractual terms which apply with the service organization, and how client monitors the service organization to ensure all its responsibilities are met.

chapter

18

Auditors' reports

In this chapter

- Audit opinion.
- Modifications to the audit report.
- Opening balances and comparatives.
- Other reports.

Audit opinion

The unqualified audit report (per ISA 700), as amended by APB Bulletin 2005/4 – Auditors Reports on Financial Statements in Great Britain and Northern Ireland.

Independent Auditors' report to the Shareholders of XYZ PLC

We have audited the parent company financial statements of (name of entity) for the year ended ... which comprise [state of primary financial statements such as the Balance Sheet, the Cash Flow Statement, the Statement of Change in Shareholders' Equity] and the related notes*.

These parent company financial statements have been prepared under the accounting policies set out therein. We have also audited the information in the Directors' Remuneration Report that is described as having been audited.

We have reported separately on the group financial statements of (name of entity) for the year ended ...

Respective responsibilities of directors and auditors

The directors' responsibilities for preparing the Annual Report, the Directors' Remuneration Report and the parent company financial statements in accordance with applicable law and International Financial Reporting Standards (IFRSs) as adopted for use in the European Union are set out in the Statement of Directors' Responsibilities.

Our responsibility is to audit the parent company financial statements and the part of the Directors' Remuneration Report to be audited in accordance with relevant legal and regulatory requirements and International Standards on Auditing (UK and Ireland).

We report to you our opinion as to whether the parent company financial statements give a true and fair view and whether the parent company financial statements and the part of the Directors' Remuneration Report to be audited have been properly prepared in accordance with the Companies Act 1985. We also report to you if, in our opinion, the Directors' Report is not consistent with the parent company financial statements, if the company has not kept proper accounting reports, if we have not received all the information and explanations we require for our audit, or if information specified by law regarding directors' remuneration and other transactions is not disclosed.

We read other information contained in the Annual Report and consider whether it is consistent with the audited parent company financial statements. The other information comprises only [the Directors' Report, the unaudited part of the Directors' Remuneration Report, the Chairman's Statement and the Operating and Financial Review]**. We consider the implications for our report if we become aware of any apparent misstatements or material inconsistencies with the parent company financial statements. Our responsibilities do not extend to any other information.

Basis of audit opinion

We conducted our audit in accordance with International Standards on Auditing (UK and Ireland) issued by the Auditing Practices Board. An audit includes examination, on a test basis, of evidence relevant to the amounts and disclosures in the parent company financial statements and the part of the Directors' Remuneration Report to be audited. It also includes an assessment of the Significant estimates and judgements made by the directors in the preparation of the parent company financial statements, and of whether the accounting policies are appropriate to the company's circumstances, consistently applied and adequately disclosed.

We planned and performed our audit so as to obtain all the information and explanations which we considered necessary in order to provide us with sufficient evidence to give reasonable assurance that the parent company financial statements and the part of the Directors' Remuneration Report to be audited are free from material misstatement, whether caused by fraud or other irregularity or error. In forming our opinion we also evaluated the overall adequacy of the presentation of information in the parent company financial statements and the part of the Directors' Remuneration Report to be audited.

Opinion

- In our opinion the parent company financial statements give a true and fair view, in accordance with IFRSs as adopted for use in the European Union as applied in the accordance with the provisions of the Companies Act 1985, of the state of the company's affairs as at ...; and
- the parent company financial statements and the part of the Directors' Remuneration Report to be audited have been properly prepared in accordance with the Companies Act 1985.

Registered auditors **Address**

Date

*Auditors' reports of entities that do not publish their financial statements on a web site or publish them using 'pdf' format, may continue to refer to the financial statements by reference to page numbers.

**The other information that is 'read' is

the content of the printed Annual Report other than the financial statements. The description of the information that has been read is tailored to reflect the terms used in the Annual Report.

Electronic communications

APB Bulletin 2001/2 encourages auditors to check electronic version of FS is identical to manually signed FS.

The APB is in the process of developing a revised version of ISA 700 and includes considerations relating to:

- guidance on forming the auditor's opinion
- supplementary information included in the FS
- date of audit report – when sufficient appropriate evidence is obtained
- conducting the audit in accordance with ISAs and National Standards
- other reporting responsibilities.

New wording part of audit report as a result.

- Better explanations of respective responsibilities.
- Updated description of the audit process reflecting the audit risk standards.
- Clarification of the scope of auditors responsibilities with respect to internal control.

Modifications to the audit report

The audit opinion may take any of the following forms:

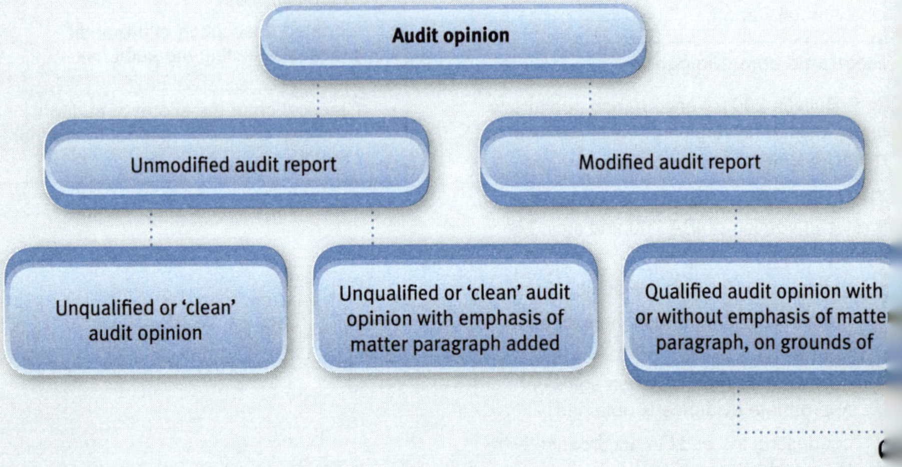

Some firms are also adding a paragraph after the opinion paragraph, disclaiming responsibility to third parties.

'Disagreement' on accounting treatment or disclosure. 'Except for' where material error **'Adverse'/'...do not show a true and fair view..'** where pervasive error

'Limitation of scope' caused by management or circumstances. 'Except for' where material error **'disclaimer'/...we are not in a position to state whether...'** where pervasive error

(1)

Significant uncertainty

Emphasis of matter an extra paragraph inserted after opinion paragraph refering to a significant mattter which is explained more fully in FS

Going concern

Opening balances and comparatives

Opening balances and comparatives

- Where there is insufficient evidence about opening balances, auditor issues on grounds of limitation of scope 'except for' where material, or 'disclaimer' where pervasive.
- Where misstatements on opening balances are not properly accounted for or disclosed then on the grounds of 'disagreement' either 'except for' or 'Adverse' opinion.

Two categories exist

Corresponding figures

- If materially misstated, audit report should be qualified.
- Where materially misstated in prior period but corrected in current period, explanatory paragraph may be appropriate.

Comparative FS included with current FS

- If opinion on one set of FS qualified, then add explanatory paragraph in current year audit report.
- Where prior year FS audited by other audito current auditor may reissue audit report on prior year or refer to fact that another audit audited prior year.
- Where prior period FS have not been audite the audit report should state the fact.

Other reports

Exam focus

- The form and content of the audit report is a highly examinable area – after all, it is the final deliverable after the planning and performance of the audit!
- Be prepared to consider if an item is material, how it affects the interpretation of the reader and, therefore whether modification to the audit report is required.
- You will also need to be in a position to describe the form and content of the other reports issued – these have already been discussed and are inserted in this chapter as triggers.

chapter 19

Reports to management

In this chapter

- Matters requiring communication.

Matters requiring communication

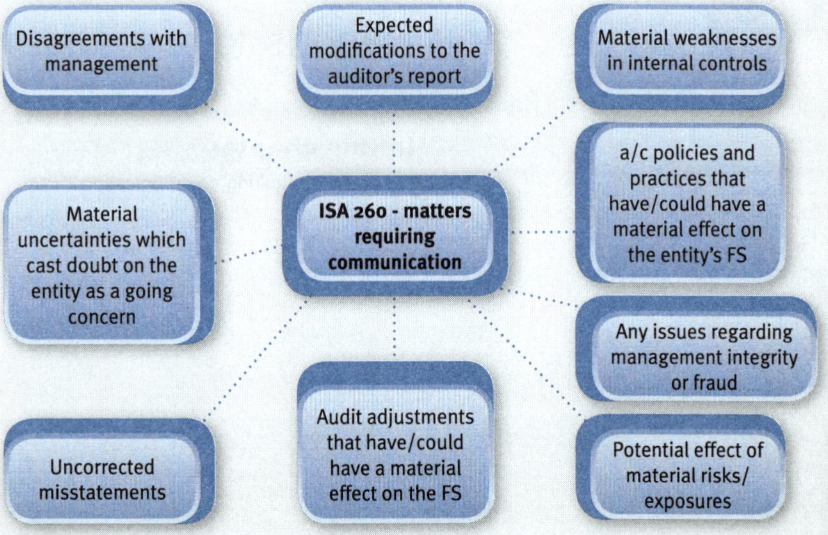

Index

A

B

C

D

E

F

G

H

I

L